THE
DOUBLE
PORTION
LIFE

THE ELISHA ANOINTING FOR
ENTERING YOUR DIVINE DESTINY

THE DOUBLE PORTION LIFE

BRUNO IERULLO

DESTINY IMAGE® PUBLISHERS, INC.

P.O. Box 310, Shippensburg, PA 17257-0310

"Promoting Inspired Lives."

This book and all other Destiny Image and Destiny Image Fiction books are available at Christian bookstores and distributors worldwide.

Cover design by Eileen Rockwell
Interior design by Terry Clifton

For more information on foreign distributors, call 717-532-3040.

Reach us on the Internet: www.destinyimage.com.

ISBN 13 TP: 978-0-7684-5737-7
ISBN 13 eBook: 978-0-7684-5738-4
ISBN 13 HC: 978-0-7684-5739-1
ISBN 13 LP: 978-0-7684-5749-0

For Worldwide Distribution, Printed in Canada
1 2 3 4 5 6 7 8 / 25 24 23 22 21

DEDICATION

THIS BOOK IS FIRST AND FOREMOST DEDICATED TO the precious Holy Spirit! I pray that the Holy Spirit impacts and anoints you as you read the pages of this book.

I also want to dedicate this book to my lovely wife, Naomi, and our five beautiful children—Hannah, Miriam, Teresa, Abigail, and John-Paul. Naomi really paid the price in the first 14 years of our marriage while we attended nightly revival meetings. In the last 30 years, Naomi's sacrifice, dedication, and unwavering commitment to walk in the love of God and then give it away to Toronto (our home city) and then to the world has been outstanding.

Last, I also dedicate this book to the ones who paved the way in my understanding of this great anointing—John and Carol Arnott. Their tenacity and their bulldog faith to remain in the anointing, to keep the anointing, and impart the anointing are unprecedented in our day. We honor these great leaders, heroes, and champions of today!

To my wife and children and John and Carol—thank you for all that I have learned through you.

CONTENTS

FOREWORD

Carol and I met Naomi when we planted our first church in Stratford, Ontario, Canada. We met Bruno in 1988, when she introduced us to him while we planted the Toronto church. It was great to see them grow in the Father's love, seeing their hearts transform and heal and walk in the love and power of the Holy Spirit.

Bruno has been in Brazil many times and traveled with me, and I traveled with him at his invitation to many nations. He has a heart for Latin-speaking nations—Italy, Argentina, and more recently France, Poland, as well as other nations.

This book is a culmination, a high point of everything that the Father has poured into us in these great days that we live in. Saying this, the prophetic promise that we recall is, "We have not seen anything yet." We believe that there is a wave of revival coming that does not end until the imminent return of Jesus.

To this end, this book is a call to seek His face, cry out for His presence, and prepare ourselves for the glory in the anointing. This is a call to all the nations and for us to be totally inundated with the transforming presence of God.

John Arnott
Toronto, Canada, 2018

PREFACE

MANY YEARS AGO, BEFORE THIS BOOK WAS EVEN imaginable, the Holy Spirit spoke to me and said, "Bruno, do you want to learn about the anointing?"

I said, "Yes, Lord," somewhat sheepishly.

The Holy Spirit responded, "Study My prophet Elijah and his predecessor." That started a journey that has not stopped; for about three years following the initial question I could almost quote the books of Kings and Samuel verse by verse from memory. I read, or should I say devoured, everything I could find on the two prophets, like Morris Cerullo's book *Passing On the Mantle*, Benny Hinn's book *The Anointing*, etc. I also traveled to Israel and the Middle East discovering the ancient paths of these prophets and to many other parts of the world where the Holy Spirit was tangibly present to learn more!

My wife was taking care of babies during the time of revival meetings, which started when the Holy Spirit was poured out in 1994 in Toronto, Canada. The image that still remains in my mind is my wife with our children all around her sometimes three to four nights a week in the church, laying hands on people and praying for more of His Spirit to come upon those receiving prayer, releasing the anointing for hundreds if not thousands of people from all over the world who were visiting us. These people were hungry and thirsty for the presence of God and would do almost anything for a touch of His presence. My wife's commitment and her sacrifice were relentless to see the Holy Spirit released in people. Her love and dedication to release me to the nations to see His Kingdom established have been and are beyond what I could ever imagine.

My wife grew up in Carol Arnott's hometown of Stratford, Ontario. She introduced me to John and Carol as they were just planting their Toronto church. In the early days when revival broke out, my wife and I joined our senior pastors John and Carol on a ministry trip. Together we went to St. John, New Brunswick to visit Pastor Steve Witt. There was a powerful move of God's Spirit in Steve's church. It was beyond what we ever encountered before—angelic visitations, people stuck to the floor of the church, unable to get up under the heavy presence of God. It was really amazing, and it was happening with children. This generation was made for these things!

That week, we ministered under the anointing of the Lord three times a day. After three days, Naomi and I started to feel tired. We were in our late 20s at the time. John and Carol asked us to take a break and we did. I can only describe the stamina in John and Carol as holy and supernatural. They were waking up early in the morning for prayer breakfast meetings and going into late hours of the night ending with revival meetings, continually releasing the anointing. They were like they were in their youth that had unlimited strength, and it was evident that it was being renewed daily. John and Carol were undoubtedly living out the promises of God (see Isa. 40:31).

Starting in those early days with John and Carol, I learned that the anointing will make a way where there is no way; it will give you strength, holy energy, and even sustain you in the midst of persecution, just as it did for the apostles in the early church.

Chapter 1

THE DOUBLE PORTION IS FOR YOU

IN JANUARY OF 1994, MANY WOULD SAY THAT THE skies opened over Canada's icy lands. The nation was shaken by the power of God. The fire of God came down. The glory of the Lord was manifested in an unusual, wonderful way. The anointing of the Holy Spirit of God touched multitudes with healings and extraordinary miracles. The hearts of men were thawed out after what we can say was a long winter. It had been a time when the life of the church was similar to a spiritual ice age with the absence of Father God's true love and embrace. But then suddenly, the flames of God fueled by compassion in liquid, tangible love took hold of Toronto, Canada and the world and released the Father's blessing!

We can say that, starting in Toronto, a splendorous and mighty outpouring of the brightness of the glory of the Lord was present. God brought forth a mighty river of healing, which expanded to the farthest parts of the earth. The worship services of extended nightly meetings were electric. Worship had become extravagant; a sweet and powerful presence invaded the atmosphere with an irresistible whirlwind of love. Because of this outpouring, Toronto was put on the world map as a place for encounter, and millions of people from all over the world came to see what was happening. Perhaps it was out of curiosity for some, but for many it was a desperate cry for more of God.

> A sweet and powerful presence invaded the atmosphere with an irresistible whirlwind of love.

For visitors it was almost impossible to stand in His presence in those early days, as many champions in faith, such as Heidi Baker, have said. It was full of heavenly glory that broke through the natural, earthly order of things.

Some also described it as the roar of the mighty Lion of the tribe of Judah. The sound of His roar was heard as a cry of restoration; people in surrender lay prostrate before the Father as they yielded themselves to the feet of Jesus. Hundreds of ministries were restored and resurrected as if from the dead. In fact, thousands of churches have been restored and countless lives were touched by the Father's love. I was privileged to be there when the heavens ripped open over us. I live in Toronto. I was there in our church four years before it started and remained there in our church throughout those extraordinary days of revival.

We saw indescribable things happen when a touch of heaven would impact the lives of hungry people who wanted more of His presence. We saw how ordinary people would receive something unusual from heaven in their lives. How the anointing made all the difference in their lives. And though we have not seen anything yet in comparison to what is yet to come—that is, the great and final outpouring of His Spirit in the last days (see Acts 2)—we were forever touched to cry out for the *more!*

How do we prepare ourselves for this next wave? I believe we should start to prepare ourselves by *thinking big*; a huge wave is coming. Biblically, I link this to the promise and His desire to release this double-portion anointing upon the earth. This book's aim is to help us long for that desire the prophet Isaiah spoke about in Isaiah 61:7: *"My people will receive twice as much wealth. Instead of being disgraced, they will be happy because of what they receive. They will receive a double share of the land"* (NCV).

I believe we should lay hold of what the prophet is expressing in the passage. Applying this to our life, the prophet is speaking about the full spectrum of the *calling over our lives*. In essence, everything in our lives has the potential to be deeply affected by the double portion.

The double portion is meant to affect *our calling* in life. This anointing is not limited, but it does mean that you can desire and expect to experience it in the following areas:

- The area of your work
- The area of your greatest influence
- The area of your gift or where you excel most

By this promise, His people, you and I, can desire to receive from the Lord great things—things we never received before, to accomplish things that we never did before or even dreamed of doing. Heidi Baker always says, "There is more, there will always be more." My prayer today is that the Holy Spirit leads us to *think big*, extravagantly far beyond what we ever imagined (see Eph. 3:20)!

ALL CHRISTIANS HAVE A CALL FROM GOD!

Leaders have been most effective when they have learned to understand their call (see Job 32:8). There are three fundamental concepts that can help us and that will make the difference in fulfilling our calling.

Destiny

To have a destiny is to walk with all your heart in what God has predestinated, said, and decreed over your life (see Jer. 29:11; Zeph. 3:17). His words over you are always good!

Mission

Your mission is to respond to His call in an undivided and humble/sincere way, learning to obey the Father's will. Much of it means seeking His Kingdom and advancing it in all nations—making disciples of all nations, baptizing, teaching, and spreading the Gospel!

Purpose

The purpose and the goal is to be 100 percent focused on doing the will of your Master. It means to be encouraged, strengthened, nourished, and supported by the Father, even in the midst of adversity.

As I studied great men and women of God, I noticed that the leaders who were the most effective in this world were those who understood the call on their lives.

> Those who were the most effective in this world were those who understood the call on their lives.

Just think of Jesus for a second. He understood His call, as the high priestly prayer reveals: *"Father, the hour has come. Glorify Your Son"* (John 17:1). We can see that Jesus absolutely operated in the anointing and knew exactly His destiny, purpose, and mission. This gave Him the strength to go from the Garden of Gethsemane to Golgotha.

The apostle Paul, who was the greatest missionary who ever lived, shadows the same heart as he says to Timothy, *"I have fought the good fight, I have finished the race, I have kept the faith"* (2 Tim. 4:7).

In summary, the call is for everyone! Destiny is yours! God gives your mission to you! And you were born for a purpose! The question is, how does this happen to you?

My goal and prayer for you in reading this book is that your life becomes full with supernatural breakthrough so that you can accomplish *great things* with your God.

The anointing is your friend and will help you achieve the above-mentioned goal. God is raising up prophets today in the spirit of Elijah and Elisha. There are keys in the lives of these two prophets that activate and put into motion this Elijah generation!

Both prophets, Elijah and Elisha, demonstrated that the anointing made the difference. Their story reveals how this new generation of prophets, anointed with a call to think big, will fulfill God's purposes in these last days. It is the anointing that really commands the blessing on our lives and ministry calling, purpose, and mission.

I have noticed that great men and women of God in history have learned the seasons or stages of their call, advancing to higher levels of anointing. Elijah and Elisha were forerunners for our sake. They were empowered and anointed by the Holy Spirit. Amazingly, even after Elisha's death he exuded/released such a powerful anointing that his dead bones resurrected a man to life when his dead body made contact in Elisha's burial cave. The anointing of the Holy Spirit is the key.

John 16:13 states, *"But when he, the Spirit of truth, comes, he will guide you into all the truth. He will not speak on his own; he will speak only what he hears, and he will tell you what is yet to come"* (NIV). Not only does the Holy Spirit reveal general future events, but He also wants to be close to you and speak specifically to us about the seasons of our lives and especially as it relates to our call.

JESUS AND THE NEW GENERATION OF PROPHETS

Jesus knew the different stages of His call in a step-by-step fashion. He knew the right time for everything because the Holy Spirit revealed it to Him. In fact, Jesus was preceded by and His way was prepared by John the Baptist, the forerunner who came in the anointing and spirit of Elijah.

The angel Gabriel appeared to Zechariah, the father of John the Baptist, and described the call in the life of his son as follows:

> *And he will turn many of the children of Israel to the Lord their God. He will also go before Him in the spirit and power of Elijah, "to turn the hearts of the fathers to the children," and the disobedient to the wisdom of the just, to make ready a people prepared for the Lord* (Luke 1:16-17).

John the Baptist fulfilled the prophecies of Elijah for his day before the first coming of the Lord Jesus.

However, Malachi prophesied that this anointing would be sent before the great and dreadful day of the Lord. After the experience of the Mount of Transfiguration, Jesus said:

> *"Tell the vision to no one until the Son of Man is risen from the dead." And His disciples asked Him, saying, "Why then do the scribes say that Elijah must come first?" Jesus answered and said to them, "Indeed, Elijah is coming first and will restore all things. But I say to you that Elijah has come already, and they did not know him but did to him whatever they wished. Likewise the Son of Man is also about to suffer at their hands." Then the disciples understood that He spoke to them of John the Baptist* (Matthew 17:9-13).

John Bevere explains in his book *The Voice of One Crying*, "Jesus spoke this after John was beheaded. Note He refers to two different time periods of the Elijah anointing: future (is coming) and past (has come)." Bevere says, "Prior to the second coming of Jesus Christ, once again God will raise a prophetic anointing. However, this time the mantle will not rest upon a single man but corporately on a group of prophets and anointed men and women in the body of Christ."[1]

> *Your sons and your daughters shall prophesy...and on My menservants and on My maidservants I will pour out My Spirit in those days; and they shall prophesy...before the coming of the great and awesome day of the Lord* (Acts 2:17-20).

This is the new, anointed generation, whose model is Jesus, that the Lord is raising in these days to *think great*.

JESUS UNDERSTOOD WHAT HE WAS ANOINTED FOR!

Jesus knew that He would grow in wisdom and stature before God and man (see Luke 2:52).

He knew that the Father commissioned Him.

He knew exactly when He had to be baptized to fulfill all righteousness.

He knew He had to go to the desert.

He knew when to begin His public ministry and announced it with the reading of Isaiah 61:

> *The Spirit of the Lord is upon Me, because He has anointed Me to preach the gospel to*

the poor; He has sent Me to heal the broken-hearted, to proclaim liberty to the captives and recovery of sight to the blind, to set at liberty those who are oppressed; to proclaim the acceptable year of the Lord (Luke 4:18-19).

Jesus knew the time of Gethsemane.

He knew the time of Golgotha.

Interestingly, because Jesus knew and learned the time of these things, wherever someone tried to pressure Him to do something before the appropriate time He remained steadfast in the Father's love for Him. He was pressured all the time but never gave up or gave in. Everything happened around His calling.

In retrospect, it is probably easy for me to outline the steps that have prepared me for the ministry of a pastor—seminary, small group leadership, service, etc. But we all need to know what our main calling is, for therein is our double-portion inheritance.

> We all need to know what our main calling is, for therein is our double-portion inheritance.

In this book, we will learn some of the different aspects of the call to ministry:

1. Preparing for the call

2. The call itself

3. Responding to the call

4. The servant's call

5. The master's call

We know that as Christians we are all called to ministry. We are not specifically speaking about holding the office of full-time ministry in the church or the marketplace. What we are talking about here is walking into an anointed lifestyle. The next several chapters are written to help us look at the foundational aspects of our lives that help set into motion the preparation for a lifestyle of ministry.

We see that many great leaders have been able to look at their lives and recognize and recall not just the actual moment they were called, how they were called, but also why they were called. John Maxwell has pointed out that the call on leaders in the Bible followed a pattern. When God decided to raise up a nation for Himself, He did not call the masses. He called a leader—Abraham. When He wanted to deliver His people from Egypt, He did not guide Israel as a group. He raised a leader to do this—Moses. When the time came to enter the Promised Land, the people followed a man—Joshua. Whenever God desired to do something great, He called a leader to take the lead. Even today He calls leaders to lead the execution of every great work. You have been called to be a part of the prophetic generation in our day.

Before we look at the different aspects in the stages of ministry mentioned above, let's look at various keys that enable us to fully surrender/yield our lives to the call, the anointing, and its transforming power.

NOTE

1. John Bevere, *The Voice of One Crying* (Palmer Lake, CO: Messenger Press, 2002), 20.

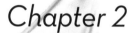

Chapter 2

THE CALL AND
THE ANOINTING

GAVE MY HEART TO THE LORD IN A DRAMATIC, life-changing experience in which I heard the Lord's audible voice saying, "If you live by the sword, you will die by the sword!" It was a voice of holiness, healing, and transformation that was able to accomplish what Jesus decreed over me, and it was the beginning of my conversion that brought me to surrender.

As that journey began, I immediately knew that God was calling me to ministry and the road that He wanted to set before me. I was willing to change to follow His path at whatever the cost. His fire consumed my whole being.

Soon after that experience, I went straight to Bible school and absorbed the Word of God; better said, I literally ate it. I was so hungry for Him that in 30 days I read the Bible from cover to cover. I was so undone by the Holy Spirit that I longed to give away what I was receiving and so I wanted to pray for people. I had a deep yearning in my heart to do the works of Jesus. I did not want anything to hold me back.

I was trying to encourage people to pray on campus, in the grocery store, and on the streets— anywhere and everywhere. I started to release what the Father gave me. I shared the good news of the

Gospel—Jesus died for our sins and rose from the dead so that we could have life.

Some of my first encounters with the Holy Spirit and His anointing were through the ministry of Derek Prince while on a Bible school ministry trip to Singapore. There were great ministries of freedom and deliverance during this trip that impacted my life. Upon my return to Canada, I was introduced to the Vineyard church mostly through attending conferences in New Brunswick. That connection with the Vineyard was how my journey involving the Toronto Vineyard church began. Prior to being married, Naomi introduced me to John Arnott in her home town of Stratford, Ontario. John asked me to attend the new Toronto church plant. The name changed as the different church locations changed. John Arnott's church was first called the Toronto Vineyard Christian Fellowship; today, it is known as Catch the Fire.

I had experienced a measure of anointing in various places around the world before the beginning of the 1994 Toronto revival, known to the world as the "Toronto Blessing." My pregnant wife and I were thrown right into the thick of ministry in those days, ministering and laying hands on the thousands who came from all over the world every night. From my estimation, the nightly meetings lasted longer than 12 years.

For Naomi and I, what we studied about in Bible school regarding revival was a reality. We felt a genuine revival break out, and it was so full of love and the presence of God.

> The glory was so heavy upon them and the rich anointing was so strong that they could not stand.

There is something I will not forget—as we served the church, we felt like we were called by and served the anointing, and in the process we saw ourselves being anointed. I will talk about this parallel with the prophet Elisha later. But in those early days, we hosted pastors in our home from all over the world. We had a van for the use of our large family of five children. When I went to church during nightly revival meetings, I often removed the bucket seats from the back of my van because people were so steeped in the presence of God that they could barely sit in the van or even physically make their way back to the van after the service. They were so gloriously debilitated under His presence. The glory was so heavy upon them and the rich anointing was so strong that they could not stand.

Many nights after the service, I had to ask friends to help me pick up these pastors and guests from the carpet on the floor. We would take them by the hands and feet and carry them up to the back of my van and then throw them like bags, on the count of three, inside the van and then close the back doors behind them. Some of them would be in the van all night in my driveway because they couldn't walk into the house. There was a time when Heidi Baker laid on the carpet under the anointing for seven whole days. All I can say is that I felt honored as these experiences brought people more deeply in love with Jesus.

The holy presence in our church caused what I call "the anointing effect." I believe that many of us, if we allow ourselves to remain soaking in His presence, will actually catch the anointing that leads us to the place of destiny.

John Arnott's definition of soaking prayer contains one of the keys to a lifestyle call to be anointed:

> Carol likes to compare soaking to making pickles. A few years ago, I found a

classical Greek word study on the Greek words *bapto*, meaning to dip, and *baptidzo*, meaning to immerse. The article used the illustration of making pickles. The recipe called for the raw fruit to be dipped in boiling water to blanch or sterilize the cucumber, using the word *bapto* which means "to dip in and out quickly." Then it called for the cucumber to be immersed, using the word *baptidzo*, and soaked in the brine and the pickling solution for several weeks.

What happens during this soaking time is that the marinade or the pickling solution soaks deep into the flesh of the cucumber until it takes on the flavor of the pickling solution so that it no longer tastes like a raw cucumber. This is what we mean by soaking. May you be so marinated in the presence of the Holy Spirit, soaking in the River of God, that you no longer "taste" like your old, raw nature any longer, but you have taken on the flavor of the Holy Spirit. "Pickle us, Lord, in the marinade of the Holy Spirit. Soak us in your wonderful presence until we become more and more like You."[1]

It was the anointing that broke the bondage of my life. It was the anointing that brought freedom to me. It was the anointing that brought favor in my life; it was the anointing that set me free, brought a greater sense of financial freedom. It was the anointing that released the blessing destined for my family and me.

I pray for you again, as you read these words, that you may be anointed as a man or woman of God. And you can pass the torch to the next generation so that we may see multitudes coming to Jesus in our day.

NOTE

1. John Arnott, "Soaking in His Presence," accessed September 15, 2020, http://srmv .convio.net/site/News2?page=NewsArticle&id =5681&news_iv_ctrl=0&abbr=art.

Chapter 3

THE TRANSFORMING POWER OF THE ANOINTING

A T THE 1994 TORONTO OUTPOURING, A WAVE OF love flooded the place. The anointing was flowing like a river. Lives were being touched with the supernatural power of God's presence—a sweet and powerful presence. Call it a simple breeze but with the force and power of a hurricane. Thousands were touched just being in the place as the weighty presence of God's glory rested on them.

Tears showered Heidi Baker's face as she heard God's heartbeat at the sound of her cry. This short, blue-eyed lady started to shine in the early hours of the morning during the seven days of her encounter. The encounter would soon, in a transformative, powerful way, cause heaven's atmosphere to send her out to Mozambique. Encounter brought personal and national transformation.

Back on the mission field, something was different. Heidi recalls a powerful meeting in the dust with the tribes of Chiure, Mozambique. Mozambique was one of the poorest nations on earth. In that meeting, blind people saw light for the first time in their lives, the deaf heard the powerful word of the Lord for the first time, and the mute worshiped the King in the beauty of His majesty. Many with their hearts broken surrendered that day to the Gospel message. There was no electricity or running water, but hundreds of people with ragged clothes and bare feet came forward. Two trucks using generators showed the film *Jesus* with overhead projectors. Hundreds of people responded to the altar calls.

In the years following, Roland Baker says, 100 percent of the deaf in the region of Chiure were healed through the power of prayer. Not only that, there are testimonies of people being raised from the dead and the multiplication of food. Because of the miracles, the Gospel has been spreading like wildfire throughout Africa. Heaven has touched earth in that place.

> 100 percent of the deaf in the region of Chiure were healed through the power of prayer.

REMEMBERING: WITHIN THE CLOUD OF GLORY

Heidi Baker was in burnout mode. At the time, she considered working at K-mart and leaving her call. I witnessed her life being radically transformed. I remember when she came from Mozambique to our church in Toronto; she was so exhausted. "I was burned out. Even though I had a doctorate in systematic theology, I did not want to teach theology," she said in a CBN news interview. "I literally wanted to work at K-mart. I was so tired."

Now, Heidi and her husband Roland lead IRIS Global, a ministry that began several thousand churches: "Jesus took the 'no' from me—the eyes, the burning eyes of Jesus. Now, I have been to 109 nations, preaching this glorious Gospel," Heidi says.

When she first came to our church, she was spiritually drained and physically ill with double pneumonia. The first thing that happened was that she was completely healed; right after the healing she had a vision. Then, "I saw Jesus—burning eyes of a burning love. God came to me."

Heidi ran to the altar, raised her hands, and started shouting, "*Yes!*" And the fire of God hit her. There was no altar call.

Randy Clark, who did not know her, said, "God wants to know if you want the nation of Mozambique."

Heidi shouted, "*Yes!*" Then the fire hit her, the power hit her. She started vibrating with power and shouted, "God, I am going to die!"

God said, "Well, I want you to die. You see, you have to die to yourself to live indeed, so you can really take the glory of God."

What happened to her? What can the anointing do? As we mentioned, it has a wonderful debilitating effect. He caused Heidi to literally fall apart like a fabric doll for a whole week. And yet it wasn't the craziest thing He did to her. Right after that, for seven days and seven nights God left her disabled. She had to be carried around by her husband. People had to bring her in and out of her hotel in Toronto on a suitcase cart. She says, "Then, they had to take me to the restroom. That was the most humiliating time of all my life."

Why would God do such a thing? Heidi said she needed to learn to love and to depend not only on Jesus but also on His people. God told her, "You can do nothing without the Body of Christ." And He caused her to be so handicapped that for seven days and seven nights she had to learn that she did not need Jesus only, she also needed His Body.

Since then, Heidi Baker's ministry has been expanding extraordinarily. Today, her organization includes well-drilling, free-of-charge health clinics for the poor, feeding programs, primary and secondary schools, and home industries. Now, more than 10,000 churches have been planted in Mozambique, and thousands of churches in more than twenty nations.

How is it that such a great and extraordinary work could be built by the ministry of this little woman and her husband? How can such an impacting and successful work be built among the people of Mozambique after innumerable attempts with no success in the mission field? No doubt the driving force of this great work is the power of the Holy Spirit and His transforming anointing.

> The driving force of this great work is the power of the Holy Spirit and His transforming anointing.

WHY SHOULD YOU DESIRE THE DOUBLE PORTION OF THE SPIRIT?

The testimony of Heidi Baker illustrates how the anointing can radically transform the call on a person's life. The anointing can deeply affect the purpose, the mission, and the destiny of a person's life!

The prophet Elisha desired the anointing with all his heart and never flinched. He had what I call a "thinking big" will! He never gave up. He experienced a huge transformation in every area of his life, expanding extraordinarily his area of influence. Before he was empowered by the anointing of the Holy Spirit, Elisha was simply a farmer who lived unknown to history. At the time, there is no mention of any miracles whatsoever being done by him. He had an absolutely ordinary life. After experiencing the double portion of the Spirit, everything changed. He jumped from just a servant lifestyle to a life marked by the supernatural.

After he was anointed, Elisha started having words of knowledge and started to see creative miracles in his life. He became a powerful prophet in his time. He was used by God to supernaturally change the course of nature, topography, weather dispositions, and see life spring forth from the dead. He prophesied the fall of the kingdoms and he ended famine and hunger. He also affected the course of economics by the power of prophecy. He directed governments, war courses/paths, and the destiny of kings. His word of command healed Naaman's leprosy, the Syrian general, besides keeping the Shunammite's family from the crisis that devastated Samaria for seven years. Elisha, who lived in the field, started being heard as a prophetic voice in palaces.

Steve Long, who has been my good friend for years, says, "There is only one Holy Spirit." The same Spirit who was upon Elisha, Peter, and Paul is the same Holy Spirit who dwells in you. And if the same Spirit who performed all these works by the prophet Elisha is dwelling in you, then you can also do what Elisha did. Desire the double portion of the Spirit with all your heart!

> The same Spirit who was upon Elisha, Peter, and Paul is the same Holy Spirit who dwells in you.

THE POWER OF THE ANOINTING

The anointing is the overflow of Christ in your life! It comes to us when we spend time in God's Word, seek Him with all our hearts, and worship Him. Jesus said:

> *If you abide in Me, and My words abide in you, you will ask what you desire, and it shall be done for you* (John 15:7).

We increase our anointing by spending time in His presence. And in time, you will begin to know when the presence of the Holy Spirit comes upon you.

REVELATION OF THE ANOINTING

I was invited to Israel to speak to a group of pastors. This was directly after the Lord asked me to learn everything possible about the anointing. From my room, I saw Bedouin shepherds roaming with their sheep. In my hand, I had a vacation Bible school lesson that my wife gave me to review and study for the following Sunday service, as she was one of the children's pastors. As I was reading the Sunday school lesson and watching the shepherds, I heard the Lord speak to me: "The anointing means to *rub*." It was like I was getting a visual, a written, and an audible message hitting me all at once. It was all revelation based.

The VBS lesson was about the practice of a shepherd anointing his sheep. As the shepherd would roam the hills and land with the sheep he loves and watches over, he would pour oil on the sheep and rub it into their wool. Stickers and other insects often got in the sheep's wool and could harm the sheep. In fact, if certain bugs entered the sheep's ears, they could get into the brain. The pain from the bugs would be so severe that the sheep would bang its skull on rocks and against trees to ease its suffering. The sheep could break its own skull seeking relief from the brain-eating parasites.

Therefore, shepherds poured oil on the head of the sheep. The oil acted as a bug repellant against the insects. They could not come near the ears because of the oily substance on the sheep's wool.

The Word of God tells us that God anoints His people with oil just as the shepherds anoint the heads of their sheep with oil. Because of this, the anointing is a symbol of blessing, protection, and strength. The anointing is our greatest weapon against the enemy's attacks.

THE MEANING OF THE ANOINTING

The Greek words for *anointing* are *chrio*—which means "blotch or rub with oil" and, by implication, "to be consecrated to the religious office or service"—and *aleipho*, which means "to anoint." In biblical times, people were anointed with oil to represent God's blessing, calling, or even comfort upon their life (see Exod. 29:7; 40:9; 2 Kings 9:6; Eccles. 9:8; James 5:14). A person was anointed for a special purpose—to be a king, to be a prophet, to be a builder, etc.

Nowadays, there is nothing wrong with anointing someone with oil. Our only concern should be that the purpose of the anointing is according to Scripture. The anointing shouldn't be seen as a magic potion. The oil has no special value in itself, unless the supernatural presence comes on the oil. Only God can anoint a person for a specific purpose. If we use the oil, it is just a symbol of what God is doing. We have seen all kinds of supernatural activity—oil being released from Bibles, through people's hands, etc.

The other meaning of the word *anointed* is "chosen." The Bible says Jesus was anointed by God with the Holy Spirit to spread the good news and set free those who were being held captives under sin (see Luke 4:18-19; Acts 10:38). After Jesus, the Christ—literally, "the anointed one"—left the earth, He gave us the gift of the Holy Spirit (see John 14:16). Now every Christian is anointed, chosen for a specific purpose, which is to promote the Kingdom of God (see 1 John 2:20).

> *Now He who establishes us with you in Christ and has anointed us is God, who also has sealed us and given us the Spirit in our hearts as a guarantee* (2 Corinthians 1:21-22).

THE MULTIPLICATION OF THE ANOINTING

In First Kings 17, we read about Elisha and the widow of Zarephath. The widow desperately needed a miracle. All she had left for her and her son was a bit of flour and a small quantity of oil to make some food. God performed a miracle that changed her life completely by multiplying her offering much beyond anything she could have dreamed. The oil and flour in the different jars did not run out until the rain came.

> When God starts moving in your life, the oil begins to flow, taking care of every need in your life.

Today, when God starts moving in your life, the oil begins to flow, taking care of every need in your life. You will not lack anything. That's what God wants for you today. He is moving powerfully on the face of the earth. When you seek Him with all your heart, the oil will flow over you, and all your desires will be met. When He is the Shepherd of your life, you lack nothing!

MULTIPLICATION SCRIPTURES AND EXAMPLES

Then God blessed them, and God said to them, "Be fruitful and multiply; fill the earth and subdue it; have dominion over the fish of the sea, over the birds of the air, and over every living thing that moves on the earth" (Genesis 1:28).

Then the Angel of the Lord called to Abraham a second time out of heaven, and said: "By Myself I have sworn...blessing I will bless you, and multiplying I will multiply your descendants as the stars of the heaven and as the sand which is on the seashore; and your descendants shall possess the gate of their enemies" (Genesis 22:15-17).

I will multiply them, and they shall not diminish; I will also glorify them, and they shall not be small (Jeremiah 30:19).

Then the churches throughout all Judea, Galilee, and Samaria had peace and were edified. And walking in the fear of the Lord and in the comfort of the Holy Spirit, they were multiplied (Acts 9:31).

SEVEN EXAMPLES OF MULTIPLICATION

1. The multiplication of the flour and oil (see 1 Kings 17:16)

2. The multiplication of wealth (see Genesis 30:35-43)

3. The multiplication of seeds (see Mark 4:26-28)

4. The multiplication of the fish and bread (see John 6:1-14)

5. The multiplication of harvest (see Genesis 26:12)

6. The multiplication of the disciples (Acts 6:7)

7. The multiplication of the oil (see 2 Kings 4:1-7)

REVIVAL MULTIPLICATION

We read in the book Acts: *"But the word of God grew and multiplied"* (Acts 12:24).

NOTE

1. Martyn Lloyd-Jones, *Revival* (Wheaton, IL: Crossway Books, 1987), 122.

Chapter 4

THINKING BIG

O N MAY 28, 1841, EDWIN MOODY DIED SUDDENLY
at 41 years of age, leaving his wife Betsy a poor
widow, in debt, with seven children, and pregnant
with her eighth. The eldest, Isaiah, was thirteen
years old; Cornelia was eleven; George, eight; Ed,
seven; Luther, six; Dwight, five; and Warren, four.
She had seven restless children to feed and clothe.
Betsy was already in her eighth month of pregnancy
when her husband died. On June 24, 1841, thinking
she was giving birth to one child she had twins, the
eighth and ninth—Samuel and Elisabeth.

Betsy Moody—at the age of 36, mother of nine
children, and a widow—was advised to give some
of her children to be raised by another family. But
although the creditors had taken the few goods she
had, she bravely launched into work, from early in
the morning to late at night. She sent the elder children to work; the others were sent to school. Betsy
cried copiously for the painful situation. Her hair
soon turned to grey. However, a certain night she
read in the Word of God: *"Leave your fatherless children, I will preserve them alive; and let your widows
trust in Me"* (Jer. 49:11). This text sustained her from
then on. In hard work in the field, that poor family
worked during the day to eat at night.

A certain day, D.L. Moody decided to leave the
fields and go to the city to try and find something

better. He gathered a few coins and went to Boston. He faced difficulties there until his uncle offered him a job in his shoe-making shop. He became an excellent shoe seller. His Sunday school teacher, Mr. Kimball, shared the Gospel with him and he gave his heart to Jesus. From Boston, D.L. Moody moved to Chicago and had great experiences with God there. The Lord started causing spiritual brokenness in him.

Moody began to think big. Like Elisha, he started desiring a new level of anointing in his life. He sought a breakthrough from the natural/mundane to the supernatural. The hunger in his heart for something greater from the Father propelled him to desire the double portion of the Spirit, which deeply affected his calling, his destiny, and his purpose.

On night while walking down the streets of New York, Moody was powerfully transformed by an encounter with God. He actually looked as if he was drunk walking down the street, but he had never drunk alcohol in his life. As he walked, every step made a decree—one foot exclaimed *glory* and the other said *hallelujah*. A cry broke through his heart: "Oh God, why don't You make me walk with You always? Set me free from myself! Absolutely possess me!"

Moody comments on this extraordinary experience when the fire of God came upon him: "Ah, what a day! I can't describe what happened to me, and rarely talk about it…what I can say is that God manifested himself to me, and I had such an experience with his love that I had to ask him to take his hand off me. I resumed preaching, my sermons were not new sermons, that is, I didn't start presenting new truths, but hundreds of people came to the Lord. I didn't want my life to go back to the way I before, even if I was offered the world as an inheritance."[1]

From then on Moody became one of the greatest evangelists of the world, expelling the kingdom of darkness from the earth.

Moody was greatly influenced by Henry Varley, who said, "The world has yet to see what God can do with a man fully consecrated to him." These words reached Moody's heart like an arrow and he became the man who impacted the United States and England with his powerful ministry, leading more than five hundred thousand people to Christ.

SPREADING THE REVIVAL FIRE

When Elijah prayed and fire came from heaven, thousands of people were converted (see 1 Kings 18).

Fire can always increase. A small sparkle can produce a great fire by adding coal or wood. In the same way, the fire of God can be imparted, and it is transferable. Revival is the holy fire that comes from heaven.

> Revival is the holy fire that comes from heaven.

Oh, that You would rend the heavens! That You would come down! That the mountains might shake at Your presence—as fire burns brushwood, as fire causes water to boil—to make Your name known to Your adversaries, that the nations may tremble at Your presence! (Isaiah 64:1-2)

My prayer is that the fire of God will increase in your life. Dr. George W. Peters said, "God, the church and the world are looking for men with burning hearts on fire—hearts full of God's love; full of compassion for the church and the world; full of passion for the glory of God, for the Gospel of Jesus Christ to go forth and bring salvation to the nations."[2]

The fire on the altar is received through prayer, and it is also fed by the Word. This is often where encounters of presence and glory will happen. And in this place, supernatural activation takes place. This fire will burn in your heart for great miracles. Wesley Duewel, in his book *Revival Fire*, describes revival in the following way: "During revival people move toward Christ. ...The very atmosphere seems awesomely filled with God's power. Christians recognize it as the holy presence of God."[3] This presence is full of flaming fire. Elisha was set ablaze with this powerful fire:

1. He always thought big; he removed small thinking from his life.

2. He was relentless in fulfilling God's call in his life.

THE DOUBLE PORTION: THINK BIG!

Elisha's initial calling is found in First Kings 19:

> *So it was, when Elijah heard it, that he wrapped his face in his mantle and went out and stood in the entrance of the cave. Suddenly a voice came to him, and said, "What are you doing here, Elijah?"*

And he said, "I have been very zealous for the Lord God of hosts; because the children of Israel have forsaken Your covenant, torn down Your altars, and killed Your prophets with the sword. I alone am left; and they seek to take my life."

Then the Lord said to him: "Go, return on your way to the Wilderness of Damascus; and when you arrive, anoint Hazael as king over Syria. Also you shall anoint Jehu the son of Nimshi as king over Israel. And Elisha the son of Shaphat of Abel Meholah you shall anoint as prophet in your place. It shall be that whoever escapes the sword of Hazael, Jehu will kill; and whoever escapes the sword of Jehu, Elisha will kill. Yet I have reserved seven thousand in Israel, all whose knees have not bowed to Baal, and every mouth that has not kissed him."

So he departed from there, and found Elisha the son of Shaphat, who was plowing with twelve yoke of oxen before him, and he was with the twelfth. Then Elijah passed by him and threw his mantle on him. And he left the oxen and ran after Elijah, and said, "Please let me kiss my father and my mother, and then I will follow you."

And he said to him, "Go back again, for what have I done to you?"

So Elisha turned back from him, and took a yoke of oxen and slaughtered them and boiled their flesh, using the oxen's equipment, and gave it to the people, and they ate. Then he arose and followed Elijah, and became his servant (1 Kings 19:13-21).

The passing of the mantle and receiving the double portion is found in Second Kings 2:

And it came to pass, when the Lord was about to take up Elijah into heaven by a whirlwind, that Elijah went with Elisha from Gilgal. Then Elijah said to Elisha, "Stay here, please, for the Lord has sent me on to Bethel."

But Elisha said, "As the Lord lives, and as your soul lives, I will not leave you!" So they went down to Bethel.

Now the sons of the prophets who were at Bethel came out to Elisha, and said to him, "Do you know that the Lord will take away your master from over you today?"

And he said, "Yes, I know; keep silent!"

Then Elijah said to him, "Elisha, stay here, please, for the Lord has sent me on to Jericho."

But he said, "As the Lord lives, and as your soul lives, I will not leave you!" So they came to Jericho.

Now the sons of the prophets who were at Jericho came to Elisha and said to him, "Do you know that the Lord will take away your master from over you today?"

So he answered, "Yes, I know; keep silent!"

Then Elijah said to him, "Stay here, please, for the Lord has sent me on to the Jordan."

But he said, "As the Lord lives, and as your soul lives, I will not leave you!" So the two of them went on. And fifty men of the sons of the prophets went and stood facing them at a distance, while the two of them stood by the Jordan. Now Elijah took his mantle, rolled it up, and struck the water; and it was divided this way and that, so that the two of them crossed over on dry ground.

And so it was, when they had crossed over, that Elijah said to Elisha, "Ask! What may I do for you, before I am taken away from you?"

Elisha said, "Please let a double portion of your spirit be upon me."

So he said, "You have asked a hard thing. Nevertheless, if you see me when I am taken from you, it shall be so for you; but if not, it shall not be so." Then it happened, as they continued on and talked, that suddenly a chariot of fire appeared with horses of fire, and separated the two of them; and Elijah went up by a whirlwind into heaven (2 Kings 2:1-11).

The verses that follow describe how Elisha picked up the mantle and entered into his double portion anointing, confirmed by a miracle—dividing the Jordan river. The Jordan itself is the place of transition:

And Elisha saw it, and he cried out, "My father, my father, the chariot of Israel and its horsemen!" So he saw him no more. And he took hold of his own clothes and tore them into two pieces. He also took up the mantle of Elijah that had fallen from him, and went back and stood by the bank of the Jordan. Then he took the mantle of Elijah that had fallen from him, and struck the water, and said, "Where is the Lord God of

Elijah?" And when he also had struck the water, it was divided this way and that; and Elisha crossed over (2 Kings 2:12-14).

OVERCOMING LIMITATIONS

Elisha did not conform to the ways of his world—just living his life working in the fields, the same old same old. He pressed on to a new level of break-through through the anointing. In some ways it does not matter who you are today; what matters is the person you are going to become when you are empowered by the Holy Spirit.

> What matters is the person you are going to become when you are empowered by the Holy Spirit.

History gives us many examples of common people who had something happen in their lives when they were anointed with power that launched them into having powerful ministries. The healing minister Smith Wigglesworth was a plumber up to 48 years of age. He was baptized with fire, and this experience changed the course of his life forever. God used him to resurrect several people from the dead; he operated with some of the most extraordinary miracles as well as prophesied what is yet to come—a revival that would change the face of Christianity in the second half of the twenty-first century.

Other great leaders were Charles and Frances Hunter. They also began their ministry later in life, in their fifties, which gives hope to many who feel they're too old to be used in a ministry capacity. After the Hunters experienced the baptism in the Holy Spirit, they started being used by God for extraordinary miracles. This wonderful couple also came to our church in Toronto and were greatly influenced by the outpouring in the '90s.

Jonathan Edwards experienced a great breakthrough in his life when he was called into ministry through an encounter with glory. He preached the famous sermon "Sinners in the Hands of an Angry God." He read his preaching notes as if they were glued to his face, held right up to his eyes, because he was short-sighted as could be. The conviction of sin gripped people so intensely that they held on to the pews they were sitting in, thinking that they were going to fall into the pit of eternal fire. No physical limitations held Edwards back.

William J. Seymour, the great leading figure of the Azusa Street revival, was a son of slaves, and Evan Roberts was just 16 years old when he led Wales to bow their knee and cry through his fiery preaching. Both these men were greatly impacted by an encounter that they later went on to say was similar to the double-portion anointing of the Spirit Elisha received.

PREPARATION TO ELISHA'S CALLING

In his commentary in the *Maxwell Leadership Bible*, John Maxwell talks about Elisha's preparation. He says Elisha was anointed to succeed Elijah. When Elisha had the opportunity to accompany Elijah, he left behind his old occupation as a farmer and adopted the vision of leadership from Elijah. The prophet Elijah found Elisha plowing the field. Elijah threw his mantle over Elisha, and the rest was history as Elisha asked if he could say farewell to his parents. He then burned his agricultural equipment. He followed Elijah wherever he went and absorbed all he could from Elijah. Maxwell says, "Mutual expectations develop naturally from mutual vision. Both Elijah and Elisha expected to do great things for God. Elisha expected and received a double portion of the anointing on Elijah."[4]

When it was near the end of Elijah's leadership, Elisha renewed his commitment with his mentor. Three times, when Elijah wanted to leave his trainee behind, Elisha answered: *"As the Lord lives, and as your soul lives, I will not leave you!"* (2 Kings 2:2).

The Bible says that Elisha performed twice as many miracles as Elijah—more miracles than any other person in the Old Testament, except for Moses.

NOTES

1. Boanerges Ribeiro, *Seara em Fogo* (CPAD), 83.

2. George W. Peters, *A Biblical Theology of Missions*, qtd. in Wesley L. Duewel, *Ablaze for God* (Candeia, 1996), 15.

3. Wesley Duewel, *Revival Fire* (Grand Rapids, MI: Zondervan), 11.

4. John Maxwell, *Maxwell Leadership Bible, New King James Version* (Nashville, TN: Thomas Nelson, 2007), 463.

Chapter 5

PREPARING
FOR THE CALL

ONCE AN ALPINIST WAS INTERVIEWED AND WAS asked the following question: "Why do you climb mountains? What motivates you to prepare, to train, to run risks, and go through pain?"

The alpinist looked at the interviewer and responded, "I see you have never been on the top of a mountain."

When we start thinking big as Elisha did, we change our perspective of the call over our lives. The perspective from the top of the mountain changes our vision of things. To get to the top of the mountain demands preparation.

THE IMPORTANCE OF PREPARATION

So he departed from there, and found Elisha the son of Shaphat, who was plowing with twelve yoke of oxen before him, and he was with the twelfth. Then Elijah passed by him and threw his mantle on him (1 Kings 19:19).

Let's focus on the first step—preparing for our calling. As the saying goes, preparation is half the battle. How was Elisha getting ready? He was plowing with the oxen—plowing to sow a big harvest!

The preparation for your calling is fundamental. It will determine how far you can get. How have you prepared? The verse really gives us hints on how he was getting ready. He was acting faithfully in the little things and dreaming with the call to something bigger.

> Preparation for your calling is fundamental. It will determine how far you can get.

Elisha was already anointed even before his calling. How do we know that? Look at how many oxen he was plowing with in the field—24 oxen in total. Note these two ways of possibly plowing the field: was it a single train of oxen or separate plows? Whatever it was, it was something huge. Elisha's 24 oxen speak of power and of volume. To top it off, Elisha himself was driving the twelfth pair!

Perhaps there is a clue in Elisha's name. *Elisha* in Hebrew means "God is salvation" or "God, your salvation." Elisha's whole life was involved in taking salvation to the nation of Israel and her surrounding nations. He lived in the period of 850 to 800 B.C.

in the northern kingdom of Israel. Elisha longed for something bigger for his life; that's why he prepared to fulfill his calling. When Elijah called him, he was ready.

Michael Phelps was the only athlete to win eight gold medals in one year in the Olympics. He broke more than 37 world records. He won 23 gold medals. He is the greatest medal winner of all time. What was his secret? He spent about 6 hours a day in a swimming pool. The time he invested in the water defined the level of victory he would reach. The apostle Paul says:

> *Don't you realize that in a race everyone runs, but only one person gets the prize? So run to win! All athletes are disciplined in their training. They do it to win a prize that will fade away, but we do it for an eternal prize.* **So I run with purpose in every step. I am not just shadowboxing. I discipline my body like an athlete, training it to do what it should** (1 Corinthians 9:24-27 NLT).

Paul ran to win the race. From the onset of our call, we run to win!

PASSING THE TEST

*And whatever you do, do it heartily, as to
the Lord and not to men* (Colossians 3:23).

Elisha passed the test to the next level. In my
life, I passed the test, so to speak, when my heart
changed in my former line of work. I was trained as a
pastor but worked in a different field. I was a super-
visor of construction and demolition; I was plodding
along in life, paying my bills, raising a family, and
doing church on Sundays. Then I had an encounter
that changed my perspective. I became determined
to be the best demolitionist in Canada and at the
same time win many for Christ, and that's what I
did. I did that with all my heart. I was really a pastor
at heart in the marketplace.

In my former career, I was called "the mil-
lion-dollar man" for bringing my company a profit
of one million dollars in a 15-minute single pre-
sentation. But I also led many to the Lord as
opportunities for me to share Jesus came about.

Robert was a former co-worker of mine who had
his driving license suspended after drinking and
driving. In that moment of crisis, not knowing how
he would get to work and feed his family, I led him
to the Lord. As he gave his heart to Jesus, he was
instantly delivered and set free. Years later when I

saw him, his family was saved and he worked as an evangelist for Billy Graham.

OVERCOMING THE ENEMY OF YOUR CALLING

The Lord is preparing you for the amazing call on your life. You are part of this prophetic generation. John 10:10 says that the devil, the thief, comes only to steal, kill, and destroy. He is committed to destroying the plans and destiny for your life. He never wants you to embrace the plans God has for you. The enemy's task is to prevent you from coming fully into your calling. Fulfilling your calling is the greatest weapon you have against him.

> The Lord is preparing you for the amazing call on your life.

For many years, the enemy made me believe that I wasn't where I should be in life. My education did not fit in my career—my training was theological, and I was working construction. I was sitting on the shelf, just getting by.

Although I could see great things taking place in my career, internally I felt that I was just going through the motions, in survival mode from salary to salary, paycheck to paycheck. When I had a stressful week and went to church on a Sunday or during the revival meeting and heard a great sermon, I was ready to leave work and go to the mission field. Africa, here I come!

In those early years of my walk with the Lord, I felt like a square peg in a round hole. Thank God for a godly wife who helped me and still keeps me in check. In general, I needed to finish that chapter of my life well before the Lord promoted me to the next.

REFLECT

Reflect and meditate, asking the Lord to give you insight. How are you plowing your current field/land (your calling)?

Bear in mind that your sowing (preparing) will determine your harvest!

PRAY

Take 15 minutes and pray with a prayer leader.

Ask Jesus: How am I getting ready? How is the farming/sowing in my life going? Write down His answer.

Note: If you desire the double portion, you need to succeed in your current assignment. Those who are faithful in little will be faithful in much (see Luke 16:10). This is a heart principle of the Kingdom.

Chapter 6

THE CALL

WHEN GOD WANTS TO DO SOMETHING BIG, HE almost always calls someone. John Sung changed the lives of many hundreds of thousands of people. Sung was the son of a Methodist pastor. When he was seventeen years old, he left China and went to the US. He first arrived in San Francisco without speaking a single word of English. In just five years at Ohio Wesleyan University and Ohio State University, even while working to support himself, he earned his Ph.D. in chemical engineering. No one had ever done such a thing, especially while working to support himself.

He then went to seminary, and on February 10, 1927 during a time of prayer John Sung was baptized in the Holy Spirit and great power came upon him. Sung tells the story when he encountered the anointing:

> This was my spiritual birthday! Although I already believed in Jesus since my early childhood days, this new experience is a life changing one for me. ...The Holy Spirit poured onto me, just like water, on top of my head. ...The Holy Spirit continuously poured onto me wave after wave.

Prior to this encounter:

> At first it seemed that there was no way to get rid of [his sins] and that he must go to Hell...He turned to the story of the cross in Gospel of Luke 23, and as he read the story came alive. So vivid was the sight of the Savior dying for his sins that he seemed to be there at the foot of the Cross and pleading to be washed from all his sins in the precious Blood... Then he heard a voice saying, "Son, thy sins are forgiven."[1]

Sung read the Bible forty-one times in a year and a half. Prompted by the Spirit, he felt a call back to China. Taking off his western clothes and dressing in typical peasant clothing, he arrived home in China and told his father: "God has called me to become an evangelist—and gave me only fifteen years." Baptized in power, Sung started a ministry filled with healing and miracles. He started to anoint and train up leaders into ministry and was the greatest Chinese evangelist during the 1930s.

His ministry had a deep impact, specifically in China and Southeast Asia. He also was part-founder of the Municipal Assembly Church, along with Watchman Nee and others. Thousands of

Chinese came to the Lord and received the Holy Spirit through his ministry. Sung prayed for multitudes to be healed and baptized with the fire of God.

Before his death at 42 years of age, he preached two to three times a day, seven days a week, eleven months out of the year. Sung also caused a radical change in Indochina, today known as the Saigon-Cholon region, and in the Chinese community of the Philippines, Thailand, and Singapore. In 1938, Sung went to Indonesia; he left there with five thousand evangelistic teams. If we consider three persons per team, we reach a total of fifteen thousand preachers who gave their hearts to the Lord and took up the call to be a full-time evangelist.

Sung was a brilliant man. He could have been a professor, a theologian, a businessman, or a scientist. Instead, his life was marked the most by his fervent boldness in asking people to make a decision to follow Christ.

What a life when we embrace our call! This young man walked in the spirit of Elisha, and the exploits that were done through his hand were unbelievable. The greater works Jesus speaks about in John 14:12 were definitely seen in his life.

EMBRACING THE CALLING

Elisha prepared himself and embraced his calling by radically changing the course of his life. He became one of the greatest prophets of the Bible. He looked way beyond the immediate borders. There was no small thinking in him! He thought big, and he sought the double portion of the Spirit. Elisha did certain things to fulfill his calling that we can learn from. Elisha embraced the call that was over his life and recognized the moment!

> *So he departed from there, and found Elisha the son of Shaphat, who was plowing with twelve yoke of oxen before him, and he was with the twelfth. Then Elijah passed by him and threw his mantle on him. And he left the oxen and ran after Elijah, and said, "Please let me kiss my father and my mother, and then I will follow you."*
>
> *And he said to him, "Go back again, for what have I done to you?"*
>
> *So Elisha turned back from him, and took a yoke of oxen and slaughtered them and boiled their flesh, using the oxen's equipment, and gave it to the people, and they ate. Then he arose and followed Elijah, and became his servant* (1 Kings 19:19-21).

Elisha was enlisted to serve Elijah and to take up the prophetic mantle. While Elisha was plowing the soil, Elijah came and threw his mantle on him. There was no doubt Elisha was anointed to accomplish his calling/destiny!

THE BURNING CALL

John Wesley, the great revivalist of the 18th century, was called by the Lord when he was only a young boy. The revival led by John and his brother Charles Wesley, associated to George Whitefield, helped England avoid a bloody revolution that could have been similar to that which took place in France. In 1814, John Wesley's ministry extended to British Guiana in South America. That same year Wesley had 31 missionaries and 17,000 church members. By 1911, the Wesleyan church had grown to 109 missionaries and 53,000 members. John Wesley's mother Susanna was the backbone behind the ministry. In fact, thousands of other preachers were raised directly under the Wesleys and traveled under direction to diverse nations in the world.

After Wesley went to be with the Lord, 43,428 ministers had been trained and more than 7 million people had become active members of a Christian church. Conservatively speaking it is stated that by

1898 more than 25 million inhabitants of the world were influenced by Wesley's preaching.

At the age of 70, John Wesley preached an open-air meeting to over thirty thousand people without amplification and yet was heard by all in attendance. At 86 years of age, he traveled to Ireland where he preached six times a day at open-air evangelistic meetings. He preached over a hundred times in sixty different cities. A follower of Wesley was recorded to say that Wesley's spirit was as alive at such an old age as when he was 53 when he met him for the first time.

THE ANOINTING WILL MAKE A WAY FOR YOU!

The anointing will empower you to accomplish your call. God has given me the privilege of having been in many personal meetings with pastor Benny Hinn where I have had the honor of seeing the anointing in operation firsthand. In Benny's book, *The Anointing*, he defines the anointing as "the tangible reality of God's presence. The anointing is the power of God manifested, a power that goes beyond anything man is able to bring forth."[2] The anointing itself cannot be seen, but the power, its manifestations, and its effects can. It is the manifestation of God's presence in power that destroys the yoke of sin and the chains of the devil and heals and impacts the sons of God to the Christian life and to a fruitful calling.

> **It is the manifestation of God's presence in power that destroys the yoke of sin and the chains of the devil and heals and impacts the sons of God to the Christian life and to a fruitful calling.**

Sheep are very nervous animals. They only lie down if they feel comfortable—if the ground is comfortable and if the shepherd is present and they feel safe. The shepherd will find the sheep that seem to have more difficulty settling down and will pull them to his side to check their mouth, nose, and wool to see if there are any insects or illnesses. The shepherd will use the staff to examine the wool and maybe apply medicine in the sheep's nose that keeps the flock at peace and heals wounds. The shepherd regularly inspects his sheep because he doesn't want today's wound to become tomorrow's infection.

It's the same with the sheep of God's flock. When we face problems, we need the Good Shepherd to help us with them so we can find rest, enjoy our lives, and not get irritated. God's anointing will protect your heart and will help you to be steadfast in your calling. I like to think of it as your best friend. It will protect you from the enemy. However, it needs to be fresh oil, as King David said, *"I have been anointed with fresh oil"* (Ps. 92:10). And this anointing (your gift) will set you before kings (see Prov. 18:16).

Is anything hindering the call on your life? As God offers us, His sheep, a checkup as the Good Shepherd, He will help us!

As Elijah threw his mantle on Elisha, we understand Elisha received an impartation and anointing as he was called to serve Elijah. In a real sense, this was his initial ordination service or act. Our church ordination services, when people are called into full-time ministry, should not just be anointing times but impartation times.

For Elisha, this mantle was the initial anointing to an invitation—an invitation to be continually anointed by impartation. This is an incredible insight of revelation into the prophets! While Elisha served

Elijah, the anointing rubbed on him. Just as the sheep, he remained in the anointing.

REFLECT

To maintain the anointing continually we must keep the enemy away/at bay from our lives. How are you doing in this sense?

PRAY

Separate for 15 minutes and pray with an intercessor.

Ask Jesus this question and write down His answer: Am I recognizing the anointing in my life? How am I maintaining it?

NOTE

1. Leslie T. Lyall, *A Biography of John Sung* (Singapore: Armour Publishing Ltd, 1954), 42.

2. Benny Hinn, *The Anointing* (Nashville, TV: Thomas Nelson, 1997), 74.

Chapter 7

ANSWERING THE CALL

THE SCOTTISH MISSIONARY ERIC LIDDELL RAN THE Olympic race of 1924 for God. The movie *Chariots of Fire* recounts the story of how the race took place. In the movie, Liddell told his sister, "God made me fast. And when I run, I feel His pleasure." Your calling will give God pleasure, and in return you sense His pleasure over you! Many times, your calling is related to something that brings the most joy in your life.

Elisha was the prophet who always had God's perspective in life, which caused him to think big and great. His calling was tied in to succession. The mantle that was being passed on to him was his dream. It was what brought him pleasure—to be the successor of Elijah the Tishbite.

For a long time I did not understand the calling on my life. In fact, I was afraid of it. I was running, like Jonah. I was running from the best thing for my life. God, in His mercy and grace, stopped me from continuing in the wrong direction, going my own way. With an audible voice He said that I was called for Him! As I surrendered, it brought me the greatest pleasure, even in difficulty!

Where do you most feel the most joy in your life and how it is related to your calling? We are not talking about playing sports that you enjoy (unless you really feel good enough to play professionally, and that is your calling). A marketplace calling is as valid as any calling. A key word outside of *pleasure* or *passion* is *influence*. Who are you leading and what influence do you have in your call? The key is finding out what Jesus planted deep in your heart that brings you life and awakens a burning passion in you.

> The key is finding out what Jesus planted deep in your heart that brings you life and awakens a burning passion in you.

FINDING THE PLACE OF YOUR CALL

Wherever there is uncommon favor in your life and you sense you have an anointing that has the ability to increase over you—this could be your calling. God wants to anoint the calling on your life so that, ultimately, you can receive a double portion of His Spirit.

First Kings shows how Elisha responded to his calling:

So Elisha turned back from him, and took a yoke of oxen and slaughtered them and boiled their flesh, using the oxen's equipment, and gave it to the people, and they ate. Then he arose and followed Elijah, and became his servant (1 Kings 19:21).

How did Elisha answer the calling in his life? By following Elijah wholeheartedly and by recognizing the new season in his life and ending the previous one well!

Elisha pursued his calling. He ran after Elijah with all his heart! This reminds me of John and Carol Arnott, my pastors. I witnessed their hunger for God's anointing. They would stop at nothing until they had it! They went to Argentina to have Claudio Freidzon place his hands on them. He asked John, "Do you want it?" John said yes, and the response was, "Tómalo!" ("Then take it!")

When Elijah threw his mantle on Elisha with all that force (anointing and impartation), he was netting Elisha into his destiny. What a picture! Elisha said, "Let me kiss my father and mother." Elisha was not stalling or making excuses. One of Jesus' disciples did that. Instead of following, he wanted to bury his father first (see Matt. 8:21). Jesus said in Luke 9:62, *"No one, having put his hand to the plow, and looking back, is fit for the kingdom of God."*

Instead, Elisha was saying, "I love my parents, and it was excellent while I was with them serving on the farm. I'm only going to tell them the good news and bless them and honor them so as to receive their blessings as I follow Elijah—my father, the prophet." This is, in fact, another amazing picture of being released with a kiss of the father's blessing into the destiny and call upon a son (or a daughter, for that matter!).

How are you answering to the calling in your own life? What is it currently costing you?

FOLLOWING THE CALL

The surprising thing concerning Elisha is that he was so sure of his calling that he burned everything. It is all or nothing. He followed his calling without looking back. What a faith he had! How are you answering the calling in your own life? What is the price you have paid? What is it currently costing you?

How many of us try to act prudently? "If it fails, I still have plan B." Elisha did not have a plan B. Out of fear, we make plan Bs so we can go back to where we used to be. Elisha knew what was best for him. He couldn't go back to agriculture. He burned all the equipment.

The apostle Peter was called to be a fisher of men—that was his true calling. After Jesus was crucified, not understanding this and having denied Jesus three times, he went back to his old occupation as a fisherman:

> *Simon Peter, Thomas called the Twin, Nathanael of Cana in Galilee, the sons of Zebedee, and two others of His disciples were together. Simon Peter said to them, "I am going fishing." They said to him, "We are going with you also." They went out and immediately got into the boat, and that night they caught nothing* (John 21:2-3).

This is a picture of how your efforts will come to no avail if you do not remain in your anointed call. The world calls this "your element." The amazing thing about the Father's love is that even in our failure there is a second chance! Just as in Peter's case, we can have numerous chances if our heart is truly repentant!

THE COST OF THE CALL

There is a cost for the call that is upon our life that all of us must face. The amazing thing is that Jesus paid it all. Ephesians 4:8 says, *"When He ascended on high, He led captivity captive, and gave gifts to men."* He has anointed us with gifts for His Kingdom!

Before I became a pastor, I was doing very well— my wife and I owned our own home, and we had far more equity in our home than the bank had on our mortgage. I had a good-paying job that allowed Naomi to be a stay-at-home mother with all our children. When I finished my last building contract, I had numerous places to work and be hired with a decent salary to provide for my family. To top it off, I specialized in my field; my resume was like a book, and many opportunities could have presented them-selves. But I came to a place where I did not want to sign another contract to support our family. That meant I had no salary to live on, a house to pay for, and a wife and five children. People thought I was crazy! But God in His grace provided and sustained us while we lived by faith for more than a year.

At a most crucial time, an unexpected gift of $10,000 was enough to launch us and send us to full-time ministry. I was hired as an associate pastor. What I learned was that there is always financial provision for what you are called to do, as long as your heart is right with God. That is the challenge! It will cost you everything, and at the same time provision always follows the anointing!

> There is always financial provision for what you are called to do, as long as your heart is right with God.

SOAKING

Soaking literally means *immersion*. It is to dive into the waters of His presence. Intimacy with the Father in the secret place is where your calling is revealed, nurtured, sustained, and maintained! Whatever it takes, whatever the cost, guard tenaciously your time with your Father, Daddy God. Deepen your intimacy with His presence. Richard J. Foster said in his book *Celebration of Discipline*, "Superficiality is the curse of our age. The desperate need today is... for deep people."[1] Shakespeare said, "Smooth runs the water where the brook is deep."[2] Isaiah 40:31 declares: *"But those who wait on the Lord shall renew their strength; they shall mount up with wings like eagles, they shall run and not be weary, they shall walk and not faint."* Waiting and going deep are interconnected!

The Lord wants to take you to the depths of the unexplored waters of His wonderful and unsearchable love in order to discover submerged treasures. He demonstrates that there are levels of intimacy in the river of His presence that go much beyond what we are used to, whether on the margin or on the surface. It is precious to soak. These are waters that spring out of God's heart, and they are going to provide exceptional healing to your life. Soaking will bring an extraordinary adventure to your call and ministry. It will transform the swamp of your soul into a place of rest and refreshing. Your inner being will become green again because these waters come out of the sanctuary (see Ezek. 47). And from the secret place of encounter, there are much deeper levels He wants to take you.

Many great men of faith in Scripture and in history lived this life in His presence through encounters. William Booth was a man of the presence. He invested his life in days of fasting and solitude to seek the presence, and that was a non-negotiable for him—it was a lifestyle.

Frances Bevan says, "The soul is drawn into the inner chamber, and there are the wonder and the riches revealed."[3] You can only soak deep into the presence if you separate quality time to be on your own with God daily. You can start with half an hour per day and see where that leads you.

Philip Yancey tells in his book *Prayer* that during the period when the professor Henri Nouwen was at Yale, he changed his closet into a prayer room and proposed to give to the Lord quality time. "I might have a thousand things to think about while I'm in there, but the fact that I'm sitting in this physical place means I'm praying." It is a consecrated, separate place with the purpose of meeting God. Nouwen did not negotiate his time with the Lord along the years in which he was involved in the academic life. Nouwen proposed to take time aside, even if it cost him some sacrifices. "I force myself stay there for fifteen minutes. I do my best to center my mind and clear it of distracting thoughts and get down to prayer, but if after fifteen minutes I haven't been entirely successful, I say: 'Lord, this was my prayer, even all this confusion. Now I'm going back to the world."[4]

REFLECT

Somehow, finances seem to follow the anointing. How is your level of faith in God's provision for your life and calling?

PRAY

Take the necessary time to pray on your own and with an intercessory leader. Soak in prayer as you lie in His presence.

Ask Jesus these questions and write down His answer:

- Who am I following?
- Am I in transition and am I finishing well?
- Have I counted the cost? Do I have a plan B, and is it related to fear?

NOTES

1. Richard J. Foster, *Celebration of Discipline* (New York, NY: HarperCollins, 1998), 1.

2. William Shakespeare, *Henry VI* part 2, Act III, scene i.

3. Frances Bevan, *Three Friends of God*, 144. Public domain.

4. Phillip Yancy, *Prayer* (Grand Rapids, MI: Zondervan, 2006), 168.

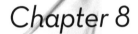

Chapter 8

THE SERVANT'S CALL

EVAN ROBERTS, LEADER OF THE GREAT REVIVAL IN
Wales, said that he was immersed in the power
of the Holy Spirit to fulfill his calling. Frank
Bartleman recalls in his book *Azusa Street* how Evan
Roberts received the double portion of the Spirit
before the revival:

> One Friday night last spring, while pray-
> ing by my bedside before retiring, I was
> taken up to a great expanse, without time
> or space. It was communion with God.
> Before this I had had a far-off God. I was
> frightened that night, but never since. So
> great was my shivering that I rocked the
> bed, and my brother, being awakened,
> took hold of me, thinking I was ill.[1]

This experience repeated every day for three
months, from one to five in the morning.

> The revival in South Wales is not of
> men, but of God. He has come very
> close to us. There is no question of creed
> or of dogma in this movement. We are
> teaching no sectarian doctrine, only the
> wonder and beauty of Christ's love. I
> have been asked concerning my meth-
> ods. I have none. I never prepare what I
> shall speak, but leave that to Him. I am

not the source of this revival, but only one agent among what is growing to be a multitude. I wish no personal following, but only the world for Christ.[2]

Roberts prophesied the rise of a generation that will be part of an unprecedented revival in history:

I believe that the world is upon the threshold of a great religious revival, and I pray daily that I may be allowed to help bring this about. Wonderful things have happened in Wales in a few weeks, but these are only a beginning. The world will be swept by His Spirit as by a rushing, mighty wind. Many who are now silent Christians will lead the movement. They will see a great light and will reflect this light to thousands now in darkness. Thousands will do more than we have accomplished, as God gives them power.[3]

This prophecy is being fulfilled. We are at the door of the greatest revival of all time, in which a new generation will rise up with a powerful calling to serve. This is the Elisha Generation, the prophets of today!

> We are at the door of the greatest revival of all time, in which a new generation will rise up with a powerful calling to serve.

THE SERVANT'S CALL

And he left the oxen and ran after Elijah, and said, "Please let me kiss my father and my mother, and then I will follow you." And he said to him, "Go back again, for what have I done to you?" (1 Kings 19:20)

How did Elisha serve and how did he benefit from it? Elisha served Elijah in the most humble way. Elisha was known for being a servant.

But Jehoshaphat said, "Is there no prophet of the Lord here, that we may inquire of the Lord by him?" So one of the servants of the king of Israel answered and said, "Elisha the son of Shaphat is here, who poured water on the hands of Elijah" (2 Kings 3:11).

We may have the wrong view of greatness, especially if we are influenced by the world's standard. Unfortunately, even in our big ministries today we look at numbers, size, etc. as if the anointing can be quantified. Let's not forget character and the heart! Jesus said, *"Just as the Son of Man did not come to be served, but to serve, and to give His life a ransom for many"* (Matt. 20:28).

THE GREATNESS OF BEING HUMBLE

There is a delusion in ministry that we are called to have great titles. Greatness comes from humility and dependency on God. The great giants of faith were always servants of all, as Paul describes himself "a chief servant."

The doctor Albert Schweitzer, who was a missionary in Africa and winner of the Nobel Prize in 1952, in speaking about ministry and one's calling affirmed, "I do not know what your destiny will be, but one thing I know: the only ones among you who will be really happy are those who will have sought and found how to serve." In 1913, he and his wife traveled to Lambarené, in French Africa. In a clinic set up in an old hen house, he started tending patients with a variety of illnesses—swamp fever, malaria, leprosy, rheumatism, open wounds, insomnia, diarrhea, and occasional cases of elephantiasis. His wife, Helen, was his nurse, and Joseph Azvawami, a native who spoke eight dialects, was his interpreter. Schweitzer's *modus operandi* was evident in the following statement: "Example is not the main thing. It is the only thing. Only as a man has simplicity can his example influence others."

THE GREATNESS OF SERVING

John Newton, the composer of the great hymn "Amazing Grace," said once:

> If two angels were to receive at the same moment a commission from God, one to go down and rule earth's grandest empire, the other to go and sweep the streets of its meanest village, it would be a matter of entire indifference to each which service fell to his lot, the post of ruler or the post of scavenger; for the joy of the angels lies only in obedience to God's will, and with equal joy they would lift a Lazarus in his rags to Abraham's bosom, or be a chariot of fire to carry an Elijah home.[4]

Second Peter 3:18 commands us to constantly be growing in grace and knowledge. It is beyond our thinking and it is radical to our culture today to think that you can earn something by serving. There is a saying that the world measures man's greatness by the number of people serving him, while heaven evaluates a man's stature by the number of people he serves. In God's economy, to think big means the opposite of what the world thinks! Jesus said, *"Yet it shall not be so among you; but whoever desires to become great among you, let him be your servant"* (Matt. 20:26). There is no escape from this. To serve is your reward. Especially when you realize Jesus was our greatest model!

To serve is your reward.

THE VALUE OF SERVING

One of the most important things I learned about the value of serving was when I worked directly for the general manager during the construction of the Toronto Airport, a project of 4.4 billion dollars. In fact, at the time this was the biggest construction project in Canada, maybe the second in North America.

The GM was a brilliant Scottish man. He taught me much about teamwork, honor, and service, and he was not even a Christian. My heart was delighted in serving him. In earlier jobs, inexperienced project managers and engineers made it difficult to serve others when their decisions involved the security and the lives of workers in demolition sites. God had to change my heart so I could honor and serve those in authority over me.

A great lesson can be learned by looking at the life of King Saul and David, his servant. David had been prophesied to be the next king. David never usurped his authority or dared to touch the Lord's anointed. In fact, David saved God's anointed from death many times over (see 1 Sam. 24–28). For me, for many years, my pride and attitude were an obstacle. I felt like I knew how to do it, my way was the only way, etc. This attitude was sabotaging the anointing upon my life. That's why I truly believe to serve well you really need to go through inner healing and deliverance ministry.

If you want the anointing upon your life to accomplish/fulfill your calling, remain humble and serve where you are! James 4:10 says, *"Humble yourselves in the sight of the Lord, and He will lift you up."*

How can you have the full anointing on your life if you are proud? The Scriptures say, *"God resists the proud, but gives grace to the humble"* (James 4:6). Let's not be deceived—the gifts and callings of God, we know, are irrevocable (see Rom. 11:29). However, that does not mean pride will not disempower the anointing on your life!

I never had a problem in serving. The real question is: who are you serving?

THE IMPORTANCE OF THE SERVANT

An interviewer asked the famous conductor Leonard Bernstein which instrument was the most difficult to play. His response was not about skill but about attitude! The conductor answered with such a presence of spirit:

> Second fiddle. I can get plenty of first violinists, but to find one who plays *second* violin with as much enthusiasm or *second* French horn or *second* flute, now that's a problem. And yet if no one plays second, we have no harmony.[5]

PRAY

Take some time on your own and with a leader to pray for humility.

And He Himself gave some to be apostles, some prophets, some evangelists, and some pastors and teachers, for the equipping of the saints for the work of ministry, for the edifying of the body of Christ (Ephesians 4:11-12).

Ask Jesus these questions and write down His answers:

- How am I serving?
- How is my anointing in serving the body of Christ?

NOTES

1. Frank Bartleman, *Azusa Street* (New Kensington, PA: Whitaker House, 1982), 31-32.
2. Ibid., 32.
3. Ibid.
4. John Newton Quotes, https://www.goodreads.com.
5. Leonard Bernstein, qtd. in Charles R. Swindoll, *Improving Your Serve* (Nashville, TN: W. Publishing Group, 1981), 35.

Chapter 9

THE MASTER'S CALL

BEING PART OF OUR CHURCH, CATCH THE FIRE, FOR almost 30 years at the writing of this book, I had the honor of being alongside great leaders such as Randy Clark, Bill Johnson, Reinhard Bonnke, and many others. When Randy Clark came to Toronto for the first time, that was a time of powerful impartation. God imparted joy, presence, prophetic gifts, etc. by the laying on of hands. We know God can work in many different ways to release the anointing. But in Toronto it was mainly through the laying on of hands. John and Carol Arnott (our spiritual parents) prayed for me several times. I have been soaked and baptized in the love of God and in His powerful anointing, which is frequently evident when you go beyond yourself to minister to others, such as going to the nations, Brazil, Italy, France, etc. Our mission is to walk in the love of God and then give it. Here is the key, as John Wimber used to say: you don't get to keep it until you give it away!

> **You don't get to keep it until you give it away!**

Heidi Baker placed her hand on my head for about an hour during a special service when she preached once. I felt waves of love coming upon me while we all sat around her in the midst of hundreds of people. When others would have hands laid on them and the anointing was present, some would shake, some would have visions, and some were even taken to heaven and so forth. I never had any outward manifestations, but I felt something powerful was released; I believed I received something. Sometimes only believing is enough. Often God uses this avenue to release His supernatural presence. That is, God is not limited but often uses human agents to impart the anointing. *Catching the fire* means what it says—God's fire is transferable.

The impartation of the anointing can come in many different ways. We talked about the anointing being imparted through the laying on of hands. One of the greatest biblical impartations was when Moses' spirit came upon the 70 elders (see Num. 11:25). In the next chapter, we shall look more specifically at Elisha's impartation.

I encourage you to gather around leaders who walk in the anointing—men and women of God— and seek something big and great from the Lord through them. Don't think small. All the leaders God used in the revival in Toronto went through stages in their call. They were servants; then they were promoted to follow the direction of Lord. They received what I call the Master's call, as Elisha did.

THE MASTER'S CALL: WAY BEYOND OURSELVES

And it came to pass, when the Lord was about to take up Elijah into heaven by a whirlwind, that Elijah went with Elisha from Gilgal. Then Elijah said to Elisha, "Stay here, please, for the Lord has sent me on to Bethel."

But Elisha said, "As the Lord lives, and as your soul lives, I will not leave you!" So they went down to Bethel.

Now the sons of the prophets who were at Bethel came out to Elisha, and said to him, "Do you know that the Lord will take away your master from over you today?"

And he said, "Yes, I know; keep silent!"

Then Elijah said to him, "Elisha, stay here, please, for the Lord has sent me on to Jericho."

But he said, "As the Lord lives, and as your soul lives, I will not leave you!" So they came to Jericho.

Now the sons of the prophets who were at Jericho came to Elisha and said to him, "Do you know that the Lord will take away your master from over you today?"

So he answered, "Yes, I know; keep silent!"

Then Elijah said to him, "Stay here, please, for the Lord has sent me on to the Jordan."

But he said, "As the Lord lives, and as your soul lives, I will not leave you!" So the two of them went on. And fifty men of the sons of the prophets went and stood facing them at a distance, while the two of them stood by the Jordan. Now Elijah took his mantle, rolled it up, and struck the water; and it was divided this way and that, so that the two of them crossed over on dry ground.

And so it was, when they had crossed over, that Elijah said to Elisha, "Ask! What may I do for you, before I am taken away from you?"

Elisha said, "Please let a double portion of your spirit be upon me."

So he said, "You have asked a hard thing. Nevertheless, if you see me when I am taken from you, it shall be so for you; but if not, it shall not be so" (2 Kings 2:1-10).

What made Elisha ask for a double-portion anointing? *Holy Spirit.*

The Holy Spirit inspired Elijah to know his time had come! Our spiritual fathers will need to understand in a similar way when their sons are to be released into the fullness of their calling. Spiritual fathers need to ask: "Has the time come?" Several times in the book of Acts we see the Holy Spirit inspiring the apostles to send out people through the laying of hands. Acts 13:1-3 is a fine example:

> *Now in the church that was at Antioch there were certain prophets and teachers: Barnabas, Simeon who was called Niger, Lucius of Cyrene, Manaen who had been brought up with Herod the tetrarch, and Saul. As they ministered to the Lord and fasted, the Holy Spirit said, "Now separate to Me Barnabas and Saul for the work to which I have called them." Then, having fasted and prayed, and laid hands on them, they sent them away.*

Elijah knew Elisha was ready for the call of the Master.

Be still before the Holy Spirit and ask Him the following questions:

- Have I prepared myself?
- Have I served well?
- Am I trustworthy?
- Have I nurtured and not squandered the anointing over my life?
- Am I going to be a father or mother of others?

As Second Kings 2:15 indicates: *"Now when the sons of the prophets who were from Jericho saw him, they said, 'The spirit of Elijah rests on Elisha.' And they came to meet him, and bowed to the ground before him."* Elisha's many years of preparation, his calling, his surrender to the anointing, and his years as a servant formed in him such tenacity and boldness that he was going to be persistent and not miss his opportunity. He followed Elijah from Gilgal, Bethel, Jericho, and then to the Jordan. These places were places of final testing; this was a school of the prophets passage/route to the office of the prophet.

Elisha was bold. He purely asked for the double-portion anointing without any pretense or false humility.

Elisha was full of passion before he was called to serve. He drove the twelfth yoke of oxen. He was apt to take up his place, casting off the old and embracing the new.

At what stage of your call are you? Where do find yourself in relation to the call of the Master?

SEEK THE DOUBLE PORTION

We know that Elisha received the double portion of Elijah's spirit because he caught the mantle when Elijah was taken up.

The "signs and wonders" that were wrought through Elisha confirmed that he received the double portion. We too can receive and have the double portion in the same way. Isaiah 61:7 declares that this is our inheritance:

> *Instead of your shame you shall have double honor, and instead of confusion they shall rejoice in their portion. Therefore in their land they shall possess double; everlasting joy shall be theirs.*

Many Bible study sources state that after reading about the spectacular life of Elijah, it is difficult to believe that any man could follow suit. However, a literal double portion of his spirit came upon Elisha's ministry. The anointing of these two prophets of God can be summarized in the following list:

ELIJAH'S LIST

1. Making rain stop for three and a half years (1 Kings 17:1)

2. Being fed by crows (1 Kings 17:4)

3. Miracle of the bin of flour and jar of oil (1 Kings 17:14)

4. The raising of the widow's son (1 Kings 17:22)

5. The calling of fire upon the altar (1 Kings 18:38)

6. Commanding rain (1 Kings 18:45)

7. Prophesying Ahab's sons would all be destroyed (1 Kings 21:22)

8. Prophesying that Jezebel would be eaten by dogs (1 Kings 21:23)

9. Prophesying that Ahaziah would die of his illness (2 Kings 1:4)

10. Calling fire from heaven upon the first 50 soldiers (1 Kings 1:10)

11. Calling fire from heaven upon the following 50 soldiers (2 Kings 1:12)

12. The parting of the Jordan (2 Kings 2:8)

13. The conditional prophecy that Elisha would have a double portion of his spirit (2 Kings 2:10)

14. Rising to heaven in a whirlwind (2 Kings 2:11)

ELISHA'S LIST

1. The parting of the Jordan (2 Kings 2:14)

2. The healing of the waters (2 Kings 2:21)

3. Calling down a curse (2 Kings 2:24)

4. The flooding of the valley with water (2 Kings 3:17)

5. Distraction of the Moabites with the valley of blood (2 Kings 3:22)

6. The miracle with the jars of oil (2 Kings 4:4)

7. Prophecy that the Shunammite woman would have a son (2 Kings 4:16)

8. Resurrection of the Shunammite's son (2 Kings 4:34)

9. Healing of the pots (2 Kings 4:41)

10. Miracle of the bread (2 Kings 4:43)

11. Healing of Naaman (2 Kings 5:14)

12. Perception of Gehazi's transgression (2 Kings 5:26)

13. Cursing of Gehazi with leprosy (2 Kings 5:27)

14. Floating of the axe head (2 Kings 6:6)

15. Prophecy regarding the Syrian battle plans (2 Kings 6:9)

16. Vision of the chariots of horses (2 Kings 6:17)

17. Attacking the Syrian army with blindness (2 Kings 6:18)

18. Restoration of the Syrian army's vision (2 Kings 6:20)

19. Prophecy regarding the end of that great famine (2 Kings 7:1)

20. Prophecy that the king of Israel would see, but not take part in the abundance (2 Kings 7:2)

21. Distraction of the Syrians with the noise of the chariots (2 Kings 7:6)

22. Prophecy regarding the seven-year famine (2 Kings 8:1)

23. Prophecy of the premature death of Ben-Hadad (2 Kings 8:10)

24. Prophecy regarding the cruelty of Hazael against Israel (2 Kings 8:12)

25. Prophecy that Jehu would strike down Ahab's house (2 Kings 9:7)

26. Prophecy that Jehoash would smite the Syrians in Aphek (2 Kings 13:17)

27. Prophecy that Jehoash would strike down Syria three times but would not consume it (2 Kings 13:19)

28. Resurrection of the dead man as he touched his bones (2 Kings 13:21)

In these last days, we are instructed to walk in our inheritance—the calling to greater works with the anointing for miracles, signs, and wonders (see John 14:12). Do you desire the same double-portion anointing? Are you hungry? Do you desire to be anointed like Elisha, whose very bones even after he died oozed out resurrection power?

So it was, as they were burying a man, that suddenly they spied a band of raiders; and they put the man in the tomb of Elisha; and when the man was let down and touched the bones of Elisha, he revived and stood on his feet (2 Kings 13:21).

MINISTRY TIME

Pray for someone and/or have someone pray for you the following as a prophetic act even if the timing is not right just yet.

- Pray for those who are not aware of their calling.
- Release the call over them.
- Pray for those who are positioned in their call so they will go forward in the Master's call and receive the double portion.
- Release the double portion.
- Make a prophetic declaration over the person.

How hungry are you to be an overcomer and be victorious? Spiritually get an arrow and shoot it until you feel the anointing come on you and you have victory over anything that is hindering your calling!

Chapter 10

ELISHA'S GENERATION IN TODAY'S TIME OF REVIVAL

IN JANUARY 1994, A SMALL CHURCH AT THE END OF the runway of Pearson International Airport in Toronto received the world's attention as a place where God had chosen to meet with His people. As a result of this divine visitation, trained members were placed in ministry teams for thousands of people from around the world to have hands laid on them so that they would receive the impartation of the Father's love and gifts.

What the British media coined as the "Toronto Blessing" became a transferable anointing in a tangible and visible form. Millions of people became overwhelmed by God's presence. People would burst out in laughing, crying, groaning, shaking, falling, drunkenness in the Spirit, and even behavior and manifestations that seemed to be pushing the envelope, like lions prophetically roaring. The outward manifestations were secondary to what God was doing in the heart; lives were forever being change and a true revival of the heart poured out on God's people!

> **The outward manifestations were secondary to what God was doing in the heart.**

The revival came suddenly and, in many ways, unexpectedly. Pastor John Arnott invited Randy Clark, a pastor from St. Louis, to minster, as John heard something took place in Randy's last leaders' meeting. What had been originally planned as a series of four meetings exploded into extended, non-stop nightly services that carried on for 12 and a half years. (After the first year, the church was closed on Mondays for one day of rest.)

By the beginning of September 1995, an estimated 600,000 visitors had come to the church, including approximately 20,000 Christian leaders and 200,000 first-time visitors from practically every charismatic denomination and country of the world. The attendance of the nightly services was peaking in the thousands and a salvation call and ministry time was offered almost every night with the help of a 45-member ministry team. Within twenty months of the outpouring of the Holy Spirit, 9,000 people had committed their lives to Christ for the very first time, and the church tripled in size to around 1,000 regular members from 360 in the beginning of 1994.

The original building, with a capacity of 425 seats, got incredibly stretched by the summer of 1994. Waiting lines started at 5 p.m. outside the doors, which were opened at 7 p.m. In November, an old conference center at Attwell Drive, east of the airport, was available to rent.

The senior pastor John Arnott signed a leasing contract to rent what was formerly the Asian Trade Centre with an option of buying. The building was purchased on January 20, 1995, exactly a year after the first day of the outpouring. The new building seated around 3,000 people and was and is very accessible to the airport's main hotels. Some hotels would offer transport service to the nightly meetings. *Toronto Life* magazine, a tourist magazine, in 1995 claimed it was the number-one tourist attraction in Toronto.

As already mentioned, the effects of the Toronto Blessing rapidly spread internationally. Within the first year, it is estimated that four thousand churches representing main denominations in the United Kingdom were touched by the renewal. One of the catalysts to the revival was Eleanor Mumford, wife of Southwest London Vineyard pastor John Mumford. The revival also broke out in May 1994 in an Anglican church, Holy Trinity Brompton, where Eleanor shared her experience in Toronto.

The Toronto Blessing spread not only to England but to Switzerland, Germany, Hungry, Norway, Korea, India, Taiwan, Thailand, Guyana

(South America), Cambodia, Australia, New Zealand, Indonesia, Malaysia, Singapore, Czech Republic, Russia, China, Kenya, Denmark, Iceland, Sweden, Romania, New Guinea, Israel, and many other countries.

CALLED TO OPERATE IN THE ANOINTING

The Toronto revival may have ebbed, but a wave of revival that would surpass/eclipse anything that was ever seen in the past has been prophesied for years.

David Ruis' Prophecy

David Ruis was leading worship at the very first Catch the Fire conference. During the worship service, David was overcome by the presence of the Holy Spirit. He had to stop playing the keyboard because his arms had begun to shake uncontrollably. After trying to control that movement for a few minutes and failing miserably, David surrendered to the Holy Spirit's prompting and began to prophesy. This is what he declared:

> I am here. I am here. I am here. Am I not He who sits in the heavens and laughs at the plans of men? Has it not already been established from time of old that My King would be established on His holy

mountain? I say to you, you thought My movement has begun. I tell you, it has yet to begin. You have seen nothing, you have seen nothing, you have seen nothing yet. This is just a preparation. You thought the seed is going out amongst the nations of the earth; I tell you that hasn't even begun. I'm just growing up a plant. My rains are coming to grow up a plant that will grow and grow and grow and then come to the place of seed. You thought you felt wind; it has been nothing. My wind shames the greatest hurricanes. My wind shames the greatest tornados. My rain and My wind wreak greater, greater, greater havoc and destruction on the realm of the enemy than any natural thing you have seen. And My wind will blow on this plant and the seeds will go forth to the nations of the earth and bring forth the greatest harvest written page or aural tongue has ever declared in the nations. Give Me glory.

You are part of this next revival generation. Just like in the days of Elijah and Elisha, we are living in times of the great manifest presence of God, not just among His people but in the whole earth (see Hab. 2:14). All of us as believers are called to operate in the anointing (see Mark 16:17-18). The Bible reveals that the anointing has power to change ordinary people into powerful weapons in the hands of the living God. When the double portion comes upon you, it will impact every area of your life. The anointing not only breaks the yoke, but also releases you to a life that God can use for His glory.

> *It shall come to pass in that day that his burden will be taken away from your shoulder, and his yoke from your neck, and the yoke will be destroyed because of the anointing oil* (Isaiah 10:27).

> *Then He called His twelve disciples together and gave them power and authority over all demons, and to cure diseases. He sent them to preach the kingdom of God and to heal the sick* (Luke 9:1-2).

THE PROMISE OF THE ANOINTING FOR THE LAST DAYS

The apostle Peter, speaking about Joel's prophecy, declares that the Holy Spirit is the great promise of God in the last days.

And it shall come to pass in the last days, says God, that I will pour out of My Spirit on all flesh; your sons and your daughters shall prophesy, your young men shall see visions, your old men shall dream dreams. And on my menservants and on my maidservants I will pour out My Spirit in those days; and they shall prophesy (Acts 2:17-18).

The anointing will enable you to heal the sick, set the captives free, and preach the Gospel of the Kingdom of God with power. Your life will become a channel of His grace!

> ## Your life will become a channel of His grace!

So, as we have highlighted, the anointing is the manifestation of God's power through His tangible presence. Reinhard Bonnke tells the story about hearing the word of the Lord come to him, saying that he would be used as a healing evangelist, only after the anointing of presence came on him. George Jeffrey, the great Welsh evangelist, said that the great secret of a man or woman powerfully used by God to change the course of history in his time is the anointing of the Holy Spirit. The anointing is the key for a life of supernatural power and miracles!

RECEIVING THE ANOINTING IN THE HIGH PLACE

He made him ride in the heights of the earth, that he might eat the produce of the fields; He made him draw honey from the rock, And oil from the flinty rock (Deuteronomy 32:13).

Just like Elisha was always thinking big and reaching for the high places, I decree prophetically that today's Elisha generation does the same and receives the double-portion anointing. A revival song brings to memory that the power of the anointing is based on God—He is a great big God and the enemy is a little bitty devil!

In John 1:50-51, Jesus promised that we would walk with Him in the supernatural and we would see heaven open. His promise to Nathaniel is our promise:

*You will see greater things than these...
Most assuredly, I say to you, hereafter you
shall see heaven open, and the angels of God*

ascending and descending upon the Son of Man.

When heaven opens upon us, we have access to a greater dimension of God's glory, broadening and expanding the level of the anointing that will manifest God's power to perform miracles, signs, and wonders.

The glory of God has dimensions and the anointing has levels. The more we get on the holy ground of God's presence and become more intimate with the Father's heart, the nearer we will be to the core of His glory (the Holy of Holies) and consequently a greater level of anointing in our lives as we position ourselves into greater atmosphere for revival. Martyn Lloyd-Jones said:

> Under the influence of this mighty power, people may literally fall to the ground under conviction of sin. ...This has frequently happened in revivals in other places, and in different centuries.[1]

This glory was seen in the days of John Wesley, George Whitefield, Jonathan Edwards, Aimee Semple McPherson, Charles Finney, William Seymour, Evan Roberts, and many modern giants of the faith, not excluding the heroes of faith in Hebrews 11.

Martyn Lloyd-Jones speaks about the impact of God's glory that occurred during the revivals. He comments that in the revival of 1859 in Northern Ireland, many remained prostrated under the weight of God's glory. Above all, the glory of God releases the breakthrough anointing for us to live a life of acceleration. The glory of God is hidden in His presence (see Isa. 6), and in it dwells the power of God. There are numberless levels of anointing in the glory of God.

> The glory of God releases the breakthrough anointing for us to live a life of acceleration.

My prayer is that the body of Christ comes into its fullness—that pure and spotless bride that is full of glory, anointed to do His will in this Elisha generation!

FINAL THOUGHTS: IMPARTATION OF THE ANOINTING

The anointing is transferable; it is imparted from one person to another. You can learn to sense the anointing as if you were holding something in your hand. You can catch the anointing, as we like to say, and place it on yourself or other people while you pray for them. The anointing is a tangible and transferable substance around you so you can minister and be used for the Kingdom of God.

> *But you have an anointing from the Holy One, and you know all things* (1 John 2:20).

> *But the anointing which you have received from Him abides in you, and you do not need that anyone teach you; but as the same anointing teaches you concerning all things, and is true, and is not a lie, and just as it has taught you, you will abide in Him* (1 John 2:27).

The anointing stays strong in us when we abide in Him, having intimacy with God the Father (see John 15). So then the call is to stay near God, remain in Him, allow Him to be the source of life in you by soaking in His presence, meditating on His Word both the *logos* and *rhema*, and resting with Him. Another great key is learning how to forgive those who have hurt us.

Intimacy really brings forth the anointing—it cultivates it, nurtures it, and sustains it and helps us to maintain a level that brings glory to God. The emphasis is really for intimacy. Power is really just the direct byproduct of the anointing. Luke 9:1 says: *"Then He called His twelve disciples together and gave them power and authority over all demons, and to cure diseases."* Most of us can see the focus in the verse as emphasizing "power and authority." However, there is a part in the verse that is glossed over. Before Jesus released the power, the verse says: *"Then He called His twelve disciples together."* He called them to Himself, away from the miraculous, and into a three-year journey of intimacy. This is the calling— we can easily have fellowship; however, to have an anointed and lasting ministry we need intimacy.

> To have an anointed and lasting ministry we need intimacy.

Let's look at and repeat three impartations in the Bible before we conclude. All three are cultivated through intimacy and are for these last days. God is raising Elisha prophets in this generation.

ELIJAH AND ELISHA

Service

Elisha was first and foremost a servant to Elijah. Elisha cooked meals, took messages, washed clothes. This gave Elisha time to build intimacy and ask Elijah questions: "Why did you...?" "Why this and why that...?" "What did you feel or see when...?"

Elisha followed Elijah everywhere in order to serve him and obey Elijah—except the day when Elijah was going to be taken to heaven. Elijah tried to separate from Elisha, but Elisha did not allow him to go. Elisha was seeking the anointing at whatever the cost!

Are you a servant of great men and women of God? Jesus was the greatest servant of all. Jesus left His royal position to serve humanity by dying on the cross.

Courage and Boldness

Elijah asked Elisha what he wanted. Elisha said the "double portion."

Can you boldly say what are you asking for? Ask and you shall receive (see Matt. 7:7)!

When God asks you, "What do you want?" be bold! *Ask*—be specific!

Ultimate Intimacy

The scene as the chariots of fire and horses came down from heaven would blow anyone's mind away! What we sometimes fail to notice in this passage is the spectacular event of the chariots and the horses only came to separate Elisha from his master, Elijah.

The miraculous and spectacular events in our lives, even though they are incredible, are not the focus. This should not be all we concentrate on. In fact, by fixing our focus on them alone we can lose the exact point of contact—the whirlwind. We need to remain focused on God and allow the supernatural to happen, but our attention needs to be keeping the main thing the main thing—that is, our worship and intimacy with our Father God.

Receiving the New

Elisha tore up his servant clothes. Yes, that was an act of rending, and this would be a meaningful way of being in mourning, but in this case it would hardly be relevant when we think of where Elijah went and how he went.

Elisha left the servant way of life to never come back. He tore that way of life apart! That does not mean he was not called to serve!

Elisha took the mantle and received the double portion. Sometimes the double portion is offered to give us authority from God, but if we don't prepare ourselves we can squander it—if we choose to be timid and allow fear to stop us. We need to be like Elisha in these last days and receive everything that is offered to us by God!

Will you receive everything that is being offered in the impartation?

PROPHETIC ACT

Take the mantle in the Spirit. Choose to receive what the Father is giving you. Say, "I receive my inheritance now."

SPIRITUAL EXERCISE

Ask a leader/pastor to prayer over you prophetically:

> *Do not neglect the gift that is in you, which was given to you by prophecy with*

the laying on of the hands of the elder-ship (1 Timothy 4:14).

Therefore I remind you to stir up the gift of God which is in you through the laying on of my hands (2 Timothy 1:6).

Paul tells Timothy stir up the gift that is in him. Similarly, remember to stir up gifts that were released in you and can be used for God's purposes!

Remember the anointing, which often comes by the impartation of the laying of hands, can last a lifetime and grow or it can last only a week and die. This is going to depend on you. If you heed the call to intimacy—Jesus is calling you to Himself—then this relationship will grow and flourish along with the anointing.

NOTE

1. Lloyd-Jones, *Revival*, 134.

EXAMPLES OF THE ANOINTING IN SCRIPTURE

But my horn shalt thou exalt like the horn of an unicorn: I shall be anointed with fresh oil (Psalm 92:10 KJV).

It was that Mary which anointed the Lord with ointment, and wiped his feet with her hair, whose brother Lazarus was sick (John 11:2 KJV).

Behold, how good and how pleasant it is for brethren to dwell together in unity! It is like the precious ointment upon the head, that ran down upon the beard, even Aaron's beard: that went down to the skirts of his garments; as the dew of Hermon, and as the dew that descended upon the mountains of Zion: for there the Lord commanded the blessing, even life for evermore (Psalm 133 KJV).

USES OF ANOINTING OIL

DECORATING A PERSON

Wash thyself therefore, and anoint thee, and put thy raiment upon thee, and get thee down to the floor: but make not thyself known unto the man, until he shall have done eating and drinking (Ruth 3:3 KJV).

FOR BURIAL

And, behold, a woman in the city, which was a sinner, when she knew that Jesus sat at meat in the Pharisee's house, brought an alabaster box of ointment, and stood at his feet behind him weeping, and began to wash his feet with tears, and did wipe them with the hairs of her head, and kissed his feet, and anointed them with the ointment (Luke 7:37-38 KJV).

For in that she hath poured this ointment on my body, she did it for my burial (Matthew 26:12 KJV).

And when the sabbath was past, Mary Magdalene, and Mary the mother of James, and Salome, had bought sweet spices, that

THE DOUBLE PORTION LIFE

they might come and anoint him (Mark 16:1 KJV).

And they returned, and prepared spices and ointments; and rested the sabbath day according to the commandment (Luke 23:56 KJV).

PURIFYING THE BODY

And thou wentest to the king with ointment, and didst increase thy perfumes, and didst send thy messengers far off, and didst debase thyself even unto hell (Isaiah 57:9 KJV).

HEALING THE SICK

And they cast out many devils, and anointed with oil many that were sick, and healed them (Mark 6:13 KJV).

Is any sick among you? let him call for the elders of the church; and let them pray over him, anointing him with oil in the name of the Lord (James 5:14 KJV).

HEALING WOUNDS

From the sole of the foot even unto the head there is no soundness in it; but wounds, and bruises, and putrifying sores: they have not been closed, neither bound up, neither mollified with ointment (Isaiah 1:6 KJV).

And went to him, and bound up his wounds, pouring in oil and wine, and set him on his own beast, and brought him to an inn, and took care of him (Luke 10:34 KJV).

PREPARING WEAPONS FOR WAR

Prepare the table, watch in the watchtower, eat, drink: arise, ye princes, and anoint the shield (Isaiah 21:5 KJV).

TO BRING JOY

Ointment and perfume rejoice the heart: so doth the sweetness of a man's friend by hearty counsel (Proverbs 27:9 KJV).

That drink wine in bowls, and anoint themselves with the chief ointments: but they are not grieved for the affliction of Joseph (Amos 6:6 KJV).

PLACES IT WAS APPLIED

ON THE HEAD

Thou preparest a table before me in the presence of mine enemies: thou anointest my head with oil; my cup runneth over (Psalm 23:5 KJV).

Let thy garments be always white; and let thy head lack no ointment (Ecclesiastes 9:8 KJV).

ON THE FACE

And wine that maketh glad the heart of man, and oil to make his face to shine, and bread which strengtheneth man's heart (Psalm 104:15 KJV).

ON THE FEET

And stood at his feet behind him weeping, and began to wash his feet with tears, and did wipe them with the hairs of her head, and kissed his feet, and anointed them with the ointment. Now when the Pharisee which had bidden him saw it, he spake within himself, saying, This man, if he were a prophet, would have known who and what manner of woman this is that toucheth him: for she is a sinner (Luke 7:38-39 KJV).

Then took Mary a pound of ointment of spikenard, very costly, and anointed the feet of Jesus, and wiped his feet with her hair: and the house was filled with the odour of the ointment (John 12:3 KJV).

ON THE EYES

I counsel thee to buy of me gold tried in the fire, that thou mayest be rich; and white raiment, that thou mayest be clothed, and that the shame of thy nakedness do not appear; and anoint thine eyes with eyesalve, that thou mayest see (Revelation 3:18 KJV).

SPIRITUAL AND MONETARY VALUES OF THE ANOINTING OIL

RICH PERFUME

Then took Mary a pound of ointment of spikenard, very costly, and anointed the feet of Jesus, and wiped his feet with her hair: and the house was filled with the odour of the ointment (John 12:3 KJV).

MORE EXPENSIVE

And Hezekiah hearkened unto them, and shewed them all the house of his precious things, the silver, and the gold, and the spices, and the precious ointment, and all the house of his armour, and all that was found in his treasures: there was nothing in his house, nor in all his dominion, that Hezekiah shewed them not (2 Kings 20:13 KJV).

That drink wine in bowls, and anoint themselves with the chief ointments: but they are not grieved for the affliction of Joseph (Amos 6:6 KJV).

Then took Mary a pound of ointment of spikenard, very costly, and anointed the feet of Jesus, and wiped his feet with her hair: and the house was filled with the odour of the ointment (John 12:3 KJV).

PREPARED BY PHARMACIST

Dead flies cause the ointment of the apothecary to send forth a stinking savour: so doth a little folly him that is in reputation for wisdom and honour (Ecclesiastes 10:1 KJV).

AN ARTICLE OF TRADE

Judah, and the land of Israel, they were thy merchants: they traded in thy market wheat of Minnith, and Pannag, and honey, and oil, and balm (Ezekiel 27:17 KJV).

And cinnamon, and odours, and ointments, and frankincense, and wine, and oil, and fine flour, and wheat, and beasts, and sheep, and horses, and chariots, and slaves, and souls of men (Revelation 18:13 KJV).

NEGLECTED IN TIMES OF AFFLICTION

Then David arose from the earth, and washed, and anointed himself, and changed his apparel, and came into the house of the Lord, and worshipped: then he came to his own house; and when he required, they set bread before him, and he did eat (2 Samuel 12:20 KJV).

And Joab sent to Tekoah, and fetched thence a wise woman, and said unto her, I pray thee, feign thyself to be a mourner, and put on now mourning apparel, and anoint not thyself with oil, but be as a woman that had a long time mourned for the dead (2 Samuel 14:2 KJV).

I ate no pleasant bread, neither came flesh nor wine in my mouth, neither did I anoint myself at all, till three whole weeks were fulfilled (Daniel 10:3 KJV).

NEGLIGENCE TO OFFER TO HOUSEGUESTS WAS A MARK OF DISRESPECT

My head with oil thou didst not anoint: but this woman hath anointed my feet with ointment (Luke 7:46 KJV).

A SIGN OF JOY

Go thy way, eat thy bread with joy, and drink thy wine with a merry heart; for God now accepteth thy works. Let thy garments be always white; and let thy head lack no ointment (Ecclesiastes 9:7-8 KJV).

DEPRIVATION, THREAT AS PUNISHMENT

Thou shalt have olive trees throughout all thy coasts, but thou shalt not anoint thyself with the oil; for thine olive shall cast his fruit (Deuteronomy 28:40 KJV).

Thou shalt sow, but thou shalt not reap; thou shalt tread the olives, but thou shalt not anoint thee with oil; and sweet wine, but shalt not drink wine (Micah 6:15 KJV).

RECOMMENDED BY CHRIST IN TIMES OF FASTING

But thou, when thou fastest, anoint thine head, and wash thy face; that thou appear not unto men to fast, but unto thy Father which is in secret: and thy Father, which seeth in secret, shall reward thee openly (Matthew 6:17-18 KJV).

AS A SYMBOL OF THE ANOINTING OF THE HOLY SPIRIT

Now he which stablisheth us with you in Christ, and hath anointed us, is God (2 Corinthians 1:21 KJV).

PEOPLE WHO RECEIVED THE ANOINTING OIL

PROPHETS

And Jehu the son of Nimshi shalt thou anoint to be king over Israel: and Elisha the son of Shaphat of Abelmeholah shalt thou anoint to be prophet in thy room (1 Kings 19:16 KJV).

The Spirit of the Lord God is upon me; because the Lord hath anointed me to preach good tidings unto the meek; he hath sent me to bind up the brokenhearted, to proclaim liberty to the captives, and the opening of the prison to them that are bound (Isaiah 61:1 KJV).

PRIESTS

And thou shalt put upon Aaron the holy garments, and anoint him, and sanctify him; that he may minister unto me in the priest's office. And thou shalt bring his sons, and clothe them with coats: And thou shalt anoint them, as thou didst anoint their father, that they may minister unto me in the priest's office: for their anointing shall surely be an everlasting priesthood throughout their generations (Exodus 40:13-15 KJV).

KINGS

The trees went forth on a time to anoint a king over them; and they said unto the olive tree, Reign thou over us (Judges 9:8 KJV).

To morrow about this time I will send thee a man out of the land of Benjamin, and thou shalt anoint him to be captain over my people Israel, that he may save my people out of the hand of the Philistines: for I have looked upon my people, because their cry is come unto me (1 Samuel 9:16 KJV).

And let Zadok the priest and Nathan the prophet anoint him there king over Israel: and blow ye with the trumpet, and say, God save king Solomon (1 Kings 1:34 KJV).

THINGS THAT WERE COVERED IN THE ANOINTING OIL

TABERNACLE AND TEMPLE

And thou shalt anoint the tabernacle of the congregation therewith, and the ark of the testimony, and the table and all his vessels, and the candlestick and his vessels, and the altar of incense (Exodus 30:26-27 KJV).

And thou shalt take the anointing oil, and anoint the tabernacle, and all that is therein, and shalt hallow it, and all the vessels thereof: and it shall be holy (Exodus 40:9 KJV).

ALTAR OF BRONZE

And thou shalt offer every day a bullock for a sin offering for atonement: and thou shalt cleanse the altar, when thou hast made an atonement for it, and thou shalt anoint it, to sanctify it (Exodus 29:36 KJV).

And thou shalt anoint the altar of the burnt offering, and all his vessels, and sanctify the altar: and it shall be an altar most holy (Exodus 40:10 KJV).

LAVER OF BRONZE

And thou shalt anoint the laver and his foot, and sanctify it (Exodus 40:11 KJV).

ABOUT BRUNO IERULLO

Bruno has been part of Catch the Fire Ministries (formerly Toronto Airport Christian Fellowship) since 1989. Since revival broke out in 1994, not only has Bruno maintained a healthy intergenerational church but has traveled to the nations carrying the fire of God!

Bruno is currently traveling the world as the Catch the Fire Ambassador of Christian Unity, reaching heads of states, nations, and the highest levels of church leadership. Training up leaders, spreading revival fire, and passionately speaking in the area of forgiveness and reconciliation are just some of the things God has placed in his heart.

Bruno is the co-chairman of United in Christ, North America and is part of the ongoing dialogue between the Emerging Charismatic churches and the Roman Catholic church. For more information, visit the website: https://www.unitedinchrist.global/. View Bruno's interview on CBN at https://www.youtube.com/watch?v=2iE99gfpXAo&feature=youtu.be.

In 2020, Bruno transitioned from Senior Pastor to Founding Pastor at Catch the Fire in Newmarket, Canada. In 2005, Bruno and his beautiful wife,

Naomi, and their five children planted what is now the oldest standing Catch the Fire church out of what is commonly known as the "Toronto Blessing."

With his grasp of different languages, Bruno as speaker, author, and pastor will help equip you to live *The Double Portion Life* in the pursuit of your destiny!